10 Curious Cases

from

'P.C. BOOKEM'S CASEBOOK'

'A Crafty Cop's Curious Cases'

by

Rev. Iain Ramsden

This book is a sequel to my ~

'Tales of a Highland Minister' *Trilogy.*

1. Tales of a Highland Minister.
2. More Tales of a Highland Minister.
3. Even More Tales of a Highland Minister.

And this book ~
4. 10 of PC Bookem's Curious Cases.

I hope you enjoy this book as much as many have enjoyed the previous three. It brings the same 'Highland and Island' humour from the West Coast of Scotland.

Mealtainn!
(enjoy!)

This book is dedicated to my lovely wife, Jo, for all her help, inspiration and support.

A big 'thank you' to my school class mate, Cathy Labbett (from Kinlochleven, now in Canada) for her 'eagle-eyed' proofreading – and for spotting all my errors before it was too late. Thanks Cathy!

Special thanks go to the <u>real</u> Constable Bookem, John Malcolm, for allowing me to use his name, for his advice and for taking it all in good humour ☺. Thanks, John!

I am very grateful to a number of kind-hearted friends and proofreaders for their positivity and encouragement.

Thank you

Iain

Front cover image purchased from iStock - design created by the author.

©Iain Ramsden 2025
ISBN : 978-1-918264-26-5

Contents

The Curious Case of ~

Chapter 1 - 'The Ballachulish Bannocks'

Chapter 2 - 'The Banshee of Rannoch Moor'

Chapter 3 - 'The Illicit Still'

Chapter 4 - 'The Whisperings'

Chapter 5 - 'The Vanishing Ferryman'

Chapter 6 - 'The Body at the Blackwater Dam'

Chapter 7 - 'The Green Lady of Mamore'

Chapter 8 - 'The Seer of Tullamore'

Chapter 9 – 'The Little Rag Doll'

Chapter 10 – 'A Fine Romance'

Introduction

Many of you will remember PC John Malcolm, otherwise known as 'Bookem,' in the popular 'Tales of a Highland Minister' books. You will recall that Bookem was quite a character, honest, upright and as determined as a bloodhound when on a case.

When he was posted to the remote Island of Rhua, in the Inner Hebrides, he struck up a friendship with the new Minister, Rev. Colin Campbell, who had moved up from Glasgow to take up the post of Minister of the Parish, on the remote Island of Rhua.

You will also remember that Bookem liked a wee dram, just to be sociable, of course.

There were many tales of intrigue and hi-jinks that Bookem was involved in, on the remote Island of Rhua, such as,

The Tinker's Curse, The Haunted Croft, The Whisky Olympics, The Bothan, and a number of other fascinating cases.

However, there will be much that you *don't* know about Constable John Malcolm, aka 'Bookem', and I hope that after reading this series of short stories, you will come to know him better and know him for the gentleman that he was.

He was born in the family croft near Dervaig, on the beautiful Isle of Mull and had a brother Archie and a sister Ina.

From a very early age, John had only ever wanted to be 'a Policeman in Tobermory.'

On leaving school, he worked for a few years on the family farm, but he never gave up on his dream of being a Policeman.

After being encouraged by his sister, he sat down one night and wrote a letter to Sergeant Galbraith in Oban, explaining his wish to join the Police Force and asking how he would go about it.

Some weeks later, he received a reply inviting him to take the ferry over to Oban and come into the Police Station on Albany Street, to discuss it further.

To cut a long story short, he applied, was accepted, and after receiving Basic Training, he became a Police Constable in the Argyllshire Constabulary.

It was a proud day for him and his family.

His first posting was to Glencoe & Ballachulish, where, apart from his usual duties, he was often called upon to help with the rescue of lost mountaineers and hill walkers in the beautiful mountains of Glencoe and the surrounding area.

After 5 years, he moved 7 miles up the road to take up the village Bobby's post in Kinlochleven, and it was here that I first came across Constable Malcolm.
He was to become my local village Bobby.

Kinlochleven was an unusual village in that it was split down the middle by the river Leven which was the boundary between Inverness-shire and Argyll. So, half of the village was in Inverness-shire and the other half was in Argyll.

It had 2 Councillors and 2 Police Stations, with two Policemen. Bookem was the 'long arm of the Law' on the Argyll side, while Sgt Kenny McKenzie covered the Inverness-shire side.
For such a small village, it was well Policed!

However, it didn't stop the local characters from keeping both Bobbies on their toes! Indeed, it was not uncommon for them to call for 'back-up' on a Saturday night from the Police officers stationed in Oban!

Kinlochleven was known for its Aluminium Factory, high rainfall, midgies and an abundance of nick-names.

Such names as Spiv, Wum, Wowsie, Cocky, Shocker, Wado, Hamo, Jaykin, Sago, Tarzan, Treacle Geordie, Fleecherty and many more, were all well known characters in the village, and it was here that PC Malcolm acquired the nickname of 'Bookem' for his tendency to 'book'em first and ask questions later.' It was a name that was to stick with him throughout the rest of his career.

He was stationed in a number of places around the Islands and Highlands, and wherever he went, he was always well respected and highly thought of.

He particularly enjoyed his time on the lovely island of Islay where he was stationed at Bowmore for 5 years.
It was here that he was to acquire a healthy liking for the peaty, Islay and Jura Malt Whiskies. (*Obviously a man of good taste!*).
Being a native Gaelic speaker, he joined the local Gaelic Choir and enjoyed a number of visits to, '*Am Mòd Nàiseanta Rìoghail*' ie The Royal National Mod (aka 'The Whisky Olympics').
He regularly attended the 'Round Church' at the top of Main Street in Bowmore, so called for its circular shape, built in such a way, so it is said, that the devil couldn't hide in the corners.

Bookem was reluctant to leave Islay but was posted to the remote island of Rhua, a small Island in the Inner Hebrides, South East of Barra and North West of Tiree.

It takes a certain kind of mindset to live happily on a remote island, but being an Islander himself, Bookem settled right in from day one.

His time on Rhua was both fulfilling and rewarding.

The escapades that he and the Reverend Colin Campbell got involved in are well documented in the 'Tales of a Highland Minister' trilogy.

To his great surprise, years later, when he had 5 years left until he was due to retire, his boyhood dream was made real.

For his long and loyal service, his Senior Officers had decided to reward him by promoting him to Sergeant and transferring him to Mull, where he would finally be the 'Policeman in Tobermory' he had always dreamed of being.

It was here, some years later, that I was to have the unexpected pleasure of meeting up with him once more.

Our meeting was the strangest thing.

I had recently moved back to Mull when, one afternoon, feeling parched after all that unpacking, I wandered down to the Mishnish Arms in Tobermory, and was enjoying a 'glass' (aka a double) of my favourite Dram – Jura.

(Note : I always order a 'glass' as I feel it would be inconsiderate to harass the barmaid into pouring another dram so soon after pouring the first one).

As I was sitting at the bar, catching up on the latest news in the Oban Times, in walked a formidable looking gentleman, 6 feet 4 inches tall if he was an inch and built to match!

He looked familiar to me, but I couldn't quite place him.

He had a lovely, soft, lilting, Highland voice, a friendly demeanour and seemed to be well known by the other customers. He was greeted by the barmaid with a friendly, "Hello John, it's yourself, will you be having the usual?"

"Och well, seeing as it's yourself that's asking," was his reply.

"OK," the barmaid smiled and replied, "One glass of Jura coming right up!"

I was somewhat taken aback as that, of course, was exactly what *I* was drinking! It was then that I realised who he was, it was John Malcolm, aka 'Bookem', the village Bobby in my home village when I was a boy, and that wasn't yesterday!

"I see you are a man of good taste, John," I said.

He smiled at me and tilted his glass towards me, saying, "Slainte Mhath, mo charaid" *(Good health, my friend)*. I raised a glass to him.

"You know my name," the big man said, it was more of a statement than a question. "Have we met before?"

"Do you not remember me, John?" I teased. "You chased me often enough!"

He looked at me again. After a few minutes, the penny seemed to have dropped.

"Young Iain MacGillivray, Nancy MacGillivray's boy! Was it not yourself I caught red-handed taking the apples from the Meenister's garden in Kinlochleven?"

"Aye, the very same." I smiled at him.

"And if I remember, did you not graduate to poaching the deer on the Mamore hills with those scoundrels Keith Campbell and Donald Green?" He smiled.

"I couldn't possibly comment, John. My memory isn't what it used to be." I smiled back.

"Aye, you wouldn't want to be bringing a discriminating against yourself!" He said with a smile. "Will you take a dram?"

"Well, seeing as it's yourself that's asking," I replied, and we both laughed.

That was to be the start of a long and close friendship between us.

We would regularly meet in the Mishnish and share a sociable *glass* or two.

I spent many a winter's night sitting by the open fire and enjoying a dram, listening to John recalling some of his many exploits, and I learned a lot about him during those years.

I learned that his favourite Bible Reading was Philippians Chapter 4, verses 4 to 9,

"*4 Rejoice in the Lord always. I will say it again: Rejoice, 5 Let your gentleness be evident to all. The Lord is near. 6 Do not be anxious about anything, but in every situation, by prayer, petition, and with thanksgiving, present your requests to God. 7 And the peace of God, which transcends all understanding, will guard your hearts and your minds in Christ Jesus.*

Finally, brothers and sisters, whatever is true, whatever is noble, whatever is right, whatever is pure, whatever is lovely, whatever is admirable – if anything is excellent or praiseworthy, think about such things. 9 Whatever you have learned or received or heard from me or seen in me – put it into practice. And the God of peace will be with you."

I learned, too, that he used these words as guide to his own life, and I learned that he was a good, honest, dependable man.

I also learned that he had an interesting 'way with words.'

Over the weeks and months, he regaled me with many fascinating stories of cases he had been involved in.
Many were everyday offences, such as poaching or alcohol related incidents, but some were, well, curious, to say the very least, and it was these more 'unusual' cases that particularly fascinated me.
I asked him if I could write some of them down for posterity, to which he reluctantly agreed.

"Aye, I don't mind you writing a line or two for *prosperity (posterity?)* – but don't go making me out to be some kind of hero, now. I was just doing my duty," he once said to me. That was typical of this humble and unassuming man.

They are not in chronological order, but in the order in which he told them to me. So, without further ado, let me pass on some of his more curious cases to you, as he gave them to me, with perhaps just a wee bit of poetic license here and there for the effect of it.

I hope I can do them justice.

So, why not pour yourself a glass of 'something medicinal,' sit back and enjoy ~

'10 Curious Cases from PC Bookem's Casebook.'

'The Curious Case of The Ballachulish Bannocks'

1.

It was a damp, dreich day in Glencoe and a veil of mist hid the tops of the hills – but that wasn't unusual for this beautiful, yet often damp, part of the Scottish Highlands.
As the locals would say, "It's the rain that makes it so bonny."

It was on a day such as this that Bookem was stirring his porridge in the Glencoe Police Station, when the telephone rang.
'Someone's early on the go today,' he thought as he lifted the receiver.
"Hello, it's the Constabulary here, Constable Malcom speaking, how can I be helping you?"
A distraught voice said, "It is myself, Peggy McLeod at Quarry Cottages in Ballachulish."
"Oh, hello Mrs McLeod, and how is your Norman's leg these days."

"Och, it's the pain in the B... (*the phone line crackled, completely obliterating her voice at that point*), "But he never complains. He's a martyr to his leg, so he is."

"Aye, just that", Bookem replied. "You sound a touch harassed if you don't mind me saying, Mrs McLeod."
"You'd be harassed too if…if…" she sobbed.
"Whatever is it, Mrs McLeod?" Bookem asked.
"It's almost too distressing to say… but… someone has stolen a tray of Bannocks that I left on a chair by the back door to cool down.
Norman is in one of his temperaments, he always has a Bannock after his porridge in the mornings.
But they've gone, that's what they are, gone!"
"And just where do you think they have gone <u>to</u>?" said PC Bookem.
"That's what *I* would like to know, Constable Malcolm. It's a mystery, so it is!"
I'll be right over, Mrs McLeod, and don't be touching anything, you could be destroying critical evidence!"

"Can I not even put on the kettle? You'll be needing a cuppa when you arrive, will you not? Is it still the four sugars that you take?"

"Well, okay then, just one cup, and be sure not to stir it as it makes it too sweet! I'll see you shortly." Bookem said and hung up.

'At last, a case!' he thought to himself as he replaced the receiver.

It had been quite some time since his role as 'upkeeper of the law' had been called upon.

There *was* that case of Mrs MacRae's Illicit Still, (See : 'The Curious Case of the Illicit Still', below), but that hadn't ended well and he preferred not to think about it.

He sharpened his pencil, picked up his notebook and made for the door. His wee dog 'Rory' followed him out and jumped up onto the passenger's seat of Bookem's Land Rover, put his front paws up on the dashboard and 'assumed the position' of both lookout and 'riding shotgun' - he was now on duty too!

It took less than 10 minutes for Bookem and his trusty sidekick, Rory, to reach Ballachulish.

Mrs McLeod was waiting for him at the door when he arrived.
"Come away in, Constable Malcolm, the kettle has just boiled."
"Hold your horses Mrs McLeod! I'll visit the crime scene first, if you don't mind, before any discriminating evidence is destroyed. *'You can't be too careful at a crime scene,'* is my motto."

"Oh well, there's the back door, and that's the chair the Bannocks were sitting on. I'll make the tea." Mrs McLeod said.

"Is Norman about?" Bookem asked.
"He's out the back, repairing a leak in the roof of the shed." Mrs McLeod replied.
"You certainly keep him busy, Mrs McLeod."

"Aye, and he's full of excuses. He says that there's no need to make a fuss, as it only leaks when it's raining!"
Bookem smiled, shook his head, and said, "Aye, he's an awful man, right enough," and he turned to survey the 'crime scene.'

He looked at the chair, then he took out his magnifying glass and inspected the back door, taking note of anything he thought might be auspicious *(suspicious?)*.

It was then that he noticed a pile of crumbs, lying on the ground.
'Aha! A clue!' Bookem said to himself, and he took a small envelope from his jacket pocket and put some of the crumbs into it.
'Aye, good detectivication is the key, I always say,' he said to himself. He had a lot of sayings like that.
He called to Mrs McLeod, "I'll take that cup of tea now, Mrs McLeod, if it's alright with yourself."
As they sat at the kitchen table, she asked,

"How are you getting on with your investigations, Constable Malcom?"

"Just grand, Mrs McLeod. Aye, just grand." He answered guardedly.

He didn't like to say too much while on a case, you never know who might be listening in from behind the scenes.

The Discrechancy is a great thing,' as he would often say.

"Well, I'd better get back on the case and thank you for the cup of tea and one of your tasty fruit scones."

"Och, it's a flatterer that you are! It's little enough for all you do for us, keeping us all safe in our beds at night," her cheeks turning a light shade of red.

"I'm just doing my duty Mrs McLeod, just doing my duty." Bookem rose and went back out to the 'scene of the crime.'

He spent the next fifteen minutes or so examining the area.

Then, he noticed a faint trail of crumbs which he followed round to the back of the Byre and over to a small wooden hut.

'Mmm, there's something dubious going on here, something very dubious indeed, Bookem said to himself as he scratched his head.

Then he heard a sound coming from the back of the hut.

"Aha! The *culprints* have returned to the scene of the crime, I've got them now!"

He crept along the side of the hut and peered around the back – but what he saw, stopped him in his tracks!

He tiptoed back to the kitchen door, "Mrs McLeod!" he whispered. "Come quick!"
"Oh, Constable Malcolm, whatever is it!?" she said as she came out of the house with a large soup ladle in her hand.

As they crept around the side of the hut, Bookem held his finger to his lips and whispered, "Shhhh, take a look, Mrs McLeod."
She lifted her ladle, ready to strike – and peeked round the corner – and there they were……

Three tiny fox cubs with their bushy tails in the air, heads down, gobbling up a pile of crumbs as their mother watched over them.

"There's your *culprints*, Mrs McLeod," Bookem said.
"Aww, the wee darlings, they're fair tucking in," she said with a big smile on her face.
"Aye, Mrs McLeod, it's testimony to your Bannocks when even the wee fox cubs enjoy them, and fox cubs are known for their good taste!" He smiled.
"Och, away with you." Mrs McLeod said as she blushed.

For the following few weeks, Mrs McLeod intentionally made a few extra Bannocks and left them out for the 'wee ones.'
After a while, the mother seemed happy to bring her cubs to the back door, and as they grew, they became quite tame.

Mr and Mrs McLeod's grandchildren were super-excited, and visits to see Granny and

Grampa were more fun than ever, thanks to the determined and dedicated detective work of PC Bookem.

*

As Constable Bookem once said ~
"Being kind brings happiness to others – and also to yourself."

Footnote :
A Scottish Bannock is a type of flatbread or cake, often made with oatmeal and other flours, and cooked on a griddle or in a pan. It's a versatile food, traditionally enjoyed with savoury dishes like stews or soups, or served sweet with butter, jam, or other toppings. Bannocks can be made with various regional variations, including fruit-filled or shortbread-like versions.
But my favourite Bannock of all, is - the 'Ballachulish Bannock!'

'The Curious Case of The Banshee of Rannoch Moor.'

2.

It was Hogmanay and the McColl family had just put up a Toast to 'Absent friends,' which was ritually given at 9 pm.
It was a cold, dark night, and the snowflakes were getting bigger. Their little, remote croft on Rannoch Moor (*just down from the Black Mount*) was lit only by the glow of the moonlight shining through the mist and reflecting off the snow.

"It's not a night for the 'Little people' to be out," Granny McColl said jokingly, as she closed over the curtains.
"That'll keep the night out," she continued, and the mood of the little family group was much improved now that the dark and menacing night had been shut out.
The table was laden with the traditional Hogmanay fare, consisting of Scotch Broth, Steak

Pie, mashed potatoes and vegetables, followed by Black Bun and Shortbread.

A dram was poured for the men, Advocaat for the ladies (*except for Granny, who always took a dram*), and lemonade for the children.

Mrs McColl loved it when her family were all home for the holidays, and they were all gathered together.

It had the makings of another enjoyable, family Hogmanay.

Midnight was getting closer as everyone readied themselves for 'the bells.'

When it was just a few minutes to midnight, they all went to the back door.

"5,4,3,2,1 Hurray!" they all shouted as Granny opened the back door and said, *"Thank you for looking after us and for all your blessings this past year,"* as she 'let the old year out.'

The little group then hurried to the front door which granny opened and said, *"Welcome New Year! Come in and may you be a good year for each of us. Bring us health and happiness."* Another 'hooray' was given and they all wished each other, 'A Happy New Year!'

Mrs McColl shed a tear – she always found Hogmanay an emotional time.

Before long, there was a tap on the window, it was Simon Fraser, their neighbour from the croft across the moor, which was about a mile away.

He had been singing Gaelic songs to keep his spirits up as he walked.

He was tall, dark and handsome, the perfect requirements for a 'First Foot,' and he had a bottle of whisky and a lump of coal in his hands.

He was their 'First Foot' of the year (the first person to set foot in their home in the New Year).

Simon and Mrs McColl's late husband, Murdo, had both been Gamekeepers on the estate for many years, and it was Simon who had found his good friend Murdo, lying lifeless on the moor, on Hogmanay, seven years before, to that very night.

"Come away in, Simon," Granny called, and once he had a dram in his hand, the party began in earnest, with Poems, Gaelic Songs, Recitations and various 'Party Pieces' – and they all sang, 'Auld Lang Syne.'

Amid all the merriment, Granny McColl was sure she could hear a voice outside – it was like someone crying. It disturbed her so much that she shouted, "Wheesht now, turn that music down! Some poor soul is crying, can you not hear it?"

Everyone stood silent for a few moments, straining their ears to hear whatever it was that Granny McColl was hearing.

"Och, mother, how many drams have you had?" Mhairi said, and they all laughed.

"That's enough of your cheek, young lady! I'm telling you, someone is crying, listen, now!"

Silence filled the room as they all looked at each other, thinking that poor Granny was havering.

But then, Seònaid (*Shona/Sheena*) said loudly, "I can hear something! It sounds like someone in pain, weeping, wailing. Oh dear, how sad she sounds, the poor soul, she must be in terrible distress."

After a moment, someone said, "Yes, I can hear it too!"

"So can I!" said another.

As they all looked at each other, Simon Fraser said, "I think I need another dram!"

"Me too," said Granny – and it was unanimously agreed that a dram was just what was needed at a time such as this.

The children ran into the room (*They had been watching the proceedings through the bedroom door, which they had quietly opened ajar*).

"There's someone outside!" Wee Morag shouted.

"We saw someone moving about on the moor, just behind the cowshed," a frightened Ceitidh (*Katie*) added.

"Okay girls, calm down now. Did you see who it was?" Granny McColl asked.

"Yes, she had long hair and looked *really* scary!" Morag gave a shiver as she spoke.

"Aye, it was really creepy," said Ceitidh.

Granny looked at Simon Fraser. "Are you thinking what I'm thinking, Simon?"

"Yes, I think I'm thinking what you're thinking," he answered. "And if I *am* thinking what you're thinking, I think we'll have to investigate. What do you think?"

"I think you're right." Granny replied.

Fortified by the copious amount of drams he had consumed, Simon stood and boldly said, "C'mon boys, let's go and find out what's going on out there!"

However, the other men weren't quite so keen to go outside.

"If you're thinking what I think you're thinking, then I think I'll stay in here!" Mhairi's husband, Iain, said.

Mhairi spoke out, "For mercy's sake, what on earth are you all talking about?

"The Banshee, Mhairi - she brings bad luck and a forewarning of death!"

"Aaaaaaah!!" the children screamed, ran into the bedroom and hid under the pile of coats on the bed which were used for extra warmth in winter.

"No-one is going anywhere," Granny said to Simon, *much to the relief of the men.*

"It's Constable Bookem that we'll be calling, he'll know what to do.

Mhairi, go through to the hall and make a telephonic call on that fancy new gadget. Be careful not to trip over the wires, I nearly took a flying header along the hallway the other day!"

"Yes, mother," Mhairi said, but she wasn't too keen on using the new contraption either.

Seònaid, being of a gentler disposition, said, "Don't worry Mhairi, I'll come with you," and the two girls left the room.

Mhairi called the operator, asking to be put through to Constable Bookem at the Police Station in Glencoe.

"He'll maybe not get through the Glen to you tonight, Mhairi," the operator said. "The snow is getting heavier, but I'll try him for you.

Oh, and how is your mother keeping? Wish her a 'Happy New Year' for me, please.
Putting you through now…"

"Hello, it's the Constabulary here, Constable Malcom speaking, how can I be helping you?"
"Oh John, it's *so* good to hear your voice again," Mhairi said.
"And who am I speaking to?"
"It's me, John, Chrissie McColl's daughter, Mhairi, up at Fraoch Croft (*Froo-chh Croit – Heather Croft*).
"Oh, mercy be! I haven't seen you since you were knee high to a midgie. How is your mother keeping just now?" Bookem asked.
"Och, she is well enough, thank you for asking, but…"
"What is it, Mhairi?"
"Well, this might sound silly but… but...
we think the Banshee is on the moor outside the croft."
"There's nothing silly about the Banshee, Mhairi I've heard her myself, it's enough to make your blood curdle!"
Bookem was concerned – the Banshee usually

only appeared when a death was imminent. He had heard her cries and wailing before – more than once – and he wasn't keen to hear her mournful weeping again.

"How is the snow with you, Mhairi?"

Mhairi pulled the curtain to one side and looked out.

"It's fair dinging down here, John, you'll not make it through the Glen tonight. Oh dear, what are we to do?" Mhairi became quite anxious.

"Don't worry now, Mhairi, I'll tell you what to do.' Bookem said.

"When I was young, the Banshee came to our neighbour, an old Cailleach who lived across the burn from us. The Banshee wailed all night, and just before dawn the wailing stopped. We thought our neighbour had passed, but at first light, there she was, out in the byre milking the cow!

My father asked her how she managed to survive the Banshee – and she told him that it was a well known fact that the Banshee can be pacified by a token of respect or a gesture of kindness. So, she offered the Banshee some of her best cream from the urn in the cow shed – and after she had drunk it, she walked away towards the shoreline and was never seen in Dervaig again."

"But we don't have any cream, John. The cow died on the very same night as our father passed on, seven years ago."

"Don't be worrying Mhairi, she will react to a gentle kindness, but it will have to be your mother or yourself who talks to her, she will only respond to another female.

Show no fear. Speak softly, respectfully and kindly – and be steadfast!

Perhaps you could offer her a shawl that has been warmed by the fire – or a bowl of warm milk or porridge that has been heated on a peat fire, to keep her warm."

"You mean… that I must go out and talk with the Banshee!? I couldn't expect mother to do it."

"Perhaps not Mhairi, but you must ask her first. It has to be *her* decision.

"Ok John," Mhairi said reluctantly. "Mother said that you would know what to do, thank you so much. Will you say a prayer for us?"

"Of course I will, and I'll get up to you at first light, if the roads are passable.
Please give your mother my best wishes – and may the good Lord watch over you all."

Mhairi relayed all that Bookem had said to her. "I'll go," said Mhairi, but her mother insisted that *she* would go out to talk to the Banshee, much to the protestations of the family.
"My 'three score and ten' years are well behind me and now every day is a blessing. You are all young and have your whole lives ahead of you. The good Lord will be with me. I put myself in *His* hands and *His* will be done."
They could see that Granny was determined to go out and wasn't going to be persuaded otherwise.
They all gave her a hug and Mhairi wrapped her mother in a warm blanket. "I love you mum," she said with a tear in her eye.

Granny McColl took a deep breath, steeled herself and went out of the back door with a mug of warm milk and a shawl, both of which had been warmed by a peat fire, just as Bookem had suggested.

Her hands were shaking, and her mind was reeling. What would she encounter? What horrors awaited her? Would she see her family again?
But she remained firm and resolute – after all, it was her family that she was protecting.

The Banshee immediately stopped wailing and stared at Granny with a confused look.
The old woman's hair was long and unkempt, down to her feet, and her face was grey, haggard and weary.

She was older than anyone or anything Granny had ever seen before, even older, she guessed, than the majestic mountain the Buachaille Etive Mhor, the 'Great Shepherd of Etive,' which has watched over the glen since time began.

Granny smiled and held out the shawl and the mug of warm milk - her courage was growing stronger by the minute.
"You must be frozen – here, take these, they will warm you," she said in Gaelic.

The Banshee looked puzzled. Was this a trick? Granny saw a blink of vulnerability, and her fear turned into pity for the old crone, destined to walk the earth for all eternity, forewarning of death. Loathed, feared and despised, wherever she went. Granny smiled at her kindly and slowly walked towards the old lady. "Here, these will keep out the cold – it's alright," she said in a comforting voice.
The Banshee was hesitant, but she must have seen the kind gesture for what it was and stretched out her hand as Granny laid the shawl over her arm and handed her the warm milk.
They looked at each other, and there was a hint of mutual respect between them.
The Banshee drank the milk, then put on the shawl – and Granny was quite sure that the

Banshee's grey and wizened face began to glow and a shadow of a smile came on her lips.

Granny nodded, smiled and walked slowly back into the croft.
The Banshee was never seen again in those parts. Maybe there *was* something in the old beliefs after all.

The family were greatly relieved to see the back door open and their beloved Granny walk back into the warmth of the kitchen, safe and unharmed.
They cheered and poured a bumper dram for each of them. Simon Fraser proposed the toast "To the bravest Granny in the world!
Good health – and a Happy New Year to us all!"
"To Granny!" they all called out.
It was the best Hogmanay that anyone could remember.
Bookem arrived at the croft about 8 o'clock the next morning and was delighted to hear that all

had gone well.

He was offered, and politely accepted a dram, just to keep out the cold, of course.

Mhairi explained how Granny had followed his good advice and spoke kindly to the Banshee.

"Your advice was a blessing, to be sure!" said Granny McColl.

"Aye," said Bookem, "the old ways are the best ways!"

And they all drank a toast to that.

As PC Bookem once said ~
*"A kind word can warm
the coldest of hearts."*

'The Curious Case of The Illicit Still'

3.

One Monday morning, just as Bookem was about to go out on a routine tour of his 'patch' in his rather rusty Land Rover, there came a knock at the door of the Glencoe Police Station. "Oh, come away in Meenister!" Bookem said, it was the Reverend Ian Russell, the local Episcopalian minister. He had come up from Edinburgh to take up the post of Minister a few months ago and was struggling with some of the 'Highland ways' of the locals.

He had been down to Edinburgh visiting family and was now back, and a meeting between the two of them was long overdue.

He and Bookem had struck up a friendship and often met at the Manse for lunch.

"I was just saying to myself that I hadn't seen you for some time," Bookem said. He was pleased to see his good friend once more.

"Yes, I've been away visiting family, but since returning, I have been made aware of a very difficult issue that I would value your thoughts on. You have a good, level head."

"And there's something I'd like <u>your</u> thoughts on too, Ian. But wait while I put on the kettle and see if I can find a biscuit or two, then we can talk."

"That sounds like a jolly good idea, John, indeed the very ticket!" said Ian rubbing his hands.

John wondered what his friend meant by, 'I've got a Ferry ticket." He knew that the ferrymen on the Ballachulish Ferry never charged himself or Ian. Perhaps it was an ecclesiastical term, so he simply replied, "Aye Ian, just that." Which seems to cover just about every situation.

They chatted freely, as good friends do, and it appears that one of the church Elders and a prominent 'pillar of the community', Mrs Fotherington, was recently lifted *(arrested)* by the

Oban Police for being drunk in charge of a pushbike.

She was seen winding her way, in an erratic manner, down the main road between Duror and Kentallen – and became abusive when a passing Police car from the Oban Force had stopped her.
"Oh dear," Bookem said, shaking his head.
"Yes indeed, but it gets worse. She then swung her handbag at Constable Galbraith, knocking off his cap, and used 'unseemly language' as they tried to bundle her into the Police car."
"Oh, my goodness! It's the devil that's in it," Bookem was shocked.
"And her a Bishop's daughter too!"
"Yes, indeed John, what would her father say? It doesn't bear thinking about"
"Would you like me to investigate, Ian? I have a friend or two in the Oban office and they might shed some light on the whole sorry situation."
"I would appreciate that John, but could you keep this 'low key,' as it were, I had her lined

up to take over as Session Clerk since poor Mr MacDonald passed on to greater glory."

"Leave it with me, and don't you worry, dischrecency is my middle name," said John tapping the side of his nose.

"Is that so? How unusual, is that a Gaelic name?"
"Um… no, och, never mind, I'll get right onto it, never you fear," replied John.
"Thank you, I know I can trust you to be discreet."
Just then, the office phone rang.
"Hello, is that yourself, Constable Malcolm?" a familiar voice said.
"Aye, it's Constable Malcolm here, is that you Fergus?"
It was Fergus McIntyre, barman in the Ballachulish Hotel, Ferry Bar.
"You'll need to come straight away. It's thon Mrs Fotherington, she's had a fair bucket (*too much to drink*) and she's up on the table doing

the can-can *(a risqué dance)* and she'll not get down.
Oh, my goodness! She's just thrown one of her surgical stockings over old Jock's head, and the boys are cheering her on. You'll have to come down or there'll be a riot soon, for sure!"
Bookem heard the cheering, it sounded like a bawdy hullabaloo right enough.

It was then that Bookem realised the time – it was only 10 o'clock in the morning!

"And just what are you doing being open at this time of the day anyway, Fergus?"
"Oh, well…er… we have some guests who are from er… from America and they are saying that it's their Interdependence Day, so we opened just to help with international relations. There's only one or two of us here, you know, to support our American cousins."

"It doesn't matter how many cousins they have in Ballachulish, it's too early for such carry-ons! I'm on my way."

Fergus hung up and told the gathering that Bookem was on his way, which prompted a mass exodus of at least 11 locals, 4 Ferrymen and 3 holiday makers.

Mrs Fotherington had fallen asleep at a table in the corner of the bar, and they couldn't waken her.
Not only that, she was snoring like a trooper!

"I'm sorry Ian, there's an emergency situation in Ballachulish." John explained.

"I'll have to go in case it turns nasty. We don't want a recurrence of what happened a few years ago," John said.
"Of course, John, you must do your duty. But what do you mean by 'a recurrence of what happened a few years ago?'"
"Och, it was a terrible thing, so it was, just terrible altogether!
There was a Wedding, the Ferryman's daughter it was, and by day three, the guests were beginning to slow down, but when Fergus

announced that they had drunk the place dry and there was no more Whisky, there was nearly a riot! I had to book-em all, all 23 of them!"

"Oh my goodness!" was all Reverend Fleming could say.

"You had better get going, John, I'll pop in to see you later in the week. By the way, what did you want to speak to me about?"

"It was about an incident in Kinlochleven, but it will have to wait for now. I'll have to go, Ian, but we'll speak later, if that is alright with yourself?"

"Of course, John, now go!"

When Bookem walked into the Ferry Bar ten minutes or so later, the place was empty, except for Fergus and Mrs Fotherington, who was still sleeping in the corner.

John knew there had recently been quite a few in the Bar before opening hours – as there were numerous dram and pint glasses lying around, and a strong smell of cigarette smoke filled the room.

"Aye Fergus, it's lucky that you are. If I didn't have Mrs Fotherington to deal with, I'd be throwing the book at you!"

He tried to wake Mrs Fotherington, but she was out cold.
He spoke loudly but to no avail, so he shook her shoulder which did the trick.
She roused and shouted irritably, "Don't manhandle me, young man! I'll call the Police on you! Constable Bookem will soon sort you out.
"Help! help!" She began to shout. "Police! Police!"
"I *AM* the Police," Bookem said to her,
slightly annoyed that she had used his nickname.
"I have no choice but to book you, Mrs Fotherington," he said as he took out his notebook and licked the end of his pencil.

"Alright now, Mrs Fotherington, what's your name?"

"But you already *know* my name – ya big daftie!" she replied.

Fergus stood behind the bar and had to turn his back for fear of Bookem seeing him laughing.

"Come on now Mrs Fotherington, I don't want to have to book you a second time for withholding vital information!"

"But you <u>*know*</u> my name!" Mrs Fotherington was getting fractious now.

As she stood up, intending to make a dash for it, an American Cream Soda bottle fell out of her shopping bag.

"What's that?" Bookem asked, he could see it was half full of a clear liquid.

"Oh, er, it's just some medicine I always carry with me." As she tried to pick it up and put it back in her bag the cap came off and its contents poured out onto the floor. It had a strong smell and Bookem knew exactly what it was – home-made whisky, otherwise known as Moonshine, Mountain Dew, or Hooch!

"Aha!" Bookem shouted. "What have we here? Where did you get this, Mrs Fotherington? You're in serious trouble now!"
She could see that the game was up and she 'spilled the beans' as they say in all the best American gangster films.

"Oh Constable Malcolm, I'm so ashamed, it has got a hold of me and I just wanted more, I couldn't help myself," and she burst into tears.

"I might be able to see my way to reducing your sentence if you tell me who you got it from."
"Sentence? You mean that I could go to jail?"
"Well, I'll do my best, but that depends on how co-operative you are." Bookem is a sly fox, right enough.

"Oh dear. What will the ladies of the Women's Guild have to say about this? I'm ruined, ruined. I'll never be able to show my face in the Ballachulish Co-op again!"

"Just tell me where you got it and I'll see what I can do, but I can't promise anything you understand."

"It was Mrs McRae up the glen, you know, at Laroch Farm, she makes it herself, out in the byre."

"Does she now? We'll see about that!
Fergus, take Mrs Fotherington home and be thankful that you're not up on a charge too!"
"A charge? For what?" Fergus was quite indignant.
"I'll think of something, now get going!"

Bookem called in to pick up one of his Special Constables, Archie McColl, who lived in Ballachulish – and the two of them headed up to Mrs McRae's Farm to see if they could find the illicit Still that Mrs Fotherington spoke about.
As they drove up the glen, they had to pull into a passing place to let a big green van go down towards the main road.

By the time they got to the Farm, Mrs McRae was outside waiting for them, had someone tipped her off?

"Oh, it's yourself Constable Malcolm, what a lovely surprise. And Archie too, how is your good lady Archie?"

"She's fine Mrs McRae, thank you for asking. Her back is still playing up but that's old age for you."

"Och how sad, but we all have our crosses to bear, will you tell her I was asking kindly for her?"

"I will, Mrs McRae, I will."

Mrs McRae was putting on a good show of being innocent, but Bookem smelled a rat *(as thon Jimmy Cagney said in one of his gangster films).*

Bookem was getting frustrated. "I'd like to inspect your byre and outer buildings this very minute, Mrs McRae."

"Of course, Constable, would you not like a cup of tea, or something a wee bit stronger, before you start?"

"No, thank you Mrs McRae, we'll start straight away if you don't mind," and he and Archie went through the sheds and the byre.
After searching high and low, no illicit paraphernalia or distilling equipment was anywhere to be seen!

"By jings, she's the fly one, right enough," said Bookem irritably.

"Did you find whatever it was you were looking for?" said Mrs McRae, innocently.
"No, we did not, as fine well you know!" Bookem was not happy.
Where could it all be?
Suddenly, Bookem and Archie looked at each other and said in unison, "The green van!" – and jumped back into the Land Rover and sped down the road, but by the time they got to the main road, there was no green van in sight.
"It could be anywhere by now," Archie said.

Bookem was frustrated – "I'll maybe have to call in the Inter-Polis," he said.

Little did they know that the green van had been driven over to Colin McIntyre's croft, just over the hill, and was hidden in his hayshed – out of sight of prying eyes.

Colin McIntyre was Fergus the Ferry barman's cousin - as well as being Mrs McRae's partner in crime.

Bookem was on the prowl, they would have to lay low – for now.

*

Bookem often quoted the saying ~

"Everything comes to you at the right moment. Be patient"

'The Curious Case of
The Whisperings'

4.

It was a typical evening in the lovely little village of Kinlochleven in Argyll, and Constable Bookem was walking over the 'short cut,' a footpath that runs alongside the river Leven and joins two sides of the village, saving a longer walk that goes, quite literally, 'around the houses.'
When I say, 'it was a typical evening in Kinlochleven', I mean that it was raining heavily and the midgies were in hiding, waiting for it to go off before coming out in full force again.

Constable Bookem was on his way to see old Mrs Devine who had recently lost her husband, Paddy. They were a lovely family and Mrs Devine was a dear soul, well liked in the village.
Not that she was often seen out and about, due to her ill health – but she had 'the gift' of seeing

and hearing things that other folk could not. Of course, that isn't unusual in the Scottish Highlands, as almost everyone knew somebody with 'the gift,' or 'the second sight.'

Mrs Devine was Bookem's 'go to' person when he was looking for help or advice on 'spiritual' matters, which arose more often than many would imagine. She also made a fair scone, so that was a major factor in Bookem's regular visits.

'Sightings,' 'happenings,' 'visions,' 'healings,' 'hearing voices' and other suchlike, were not uncommon in small Highland communities where the people lived in such close proximity with nature. Mix that with superstition and centuries of fear and misconception and you have a recipe for such beliefs – or is it all real and only comprehended by the few?

Bookem was born and brought up on a farm near Dervaig on the beautiful Island of Mull and he had seen and experienced many things that plain logic could not explain, things which were beyond even his imagining – which gave him a healthy respect for such things.

He was wise enough to know that just because _he_ couldn't understand it didn't mean it didn't exist.

Since moving up from the Glencoe Police Station to a new beat based in Kinlochleven, he was aware that many of the 'old' ways and beliefs were still alive and well.

Mrs Devine, aka Lizzie, had helped him on a number of occasions – and so, when this new and most recent matter arose, Bookem knew exactly who to turn to for help and sound advice – Lizzie Devine.

By this time, it was just beginning to get dark, and as Bookem made his way along the 'short cut,' through the trees along the well trodden footpath beside the river, his mind began to play tricks on him, or so he imagined.

Were those voices he was hearing? Or was it the guttering of the river? Perhaps it was folk

coming along the path behind him – perhaps.
For as big and experienced as Bookem was, he quickened his pace – and in a few minutes, he had reached the other side and was now standing on solid ground under the dim street lights of Wades road.

He shook his head and thought, *'Aye, the imagination is a great thing,'* and chastised himself for succumbing to such flights of fancy.

Just a few minutes later, Bookem knocked on Lizzie Devine's front door in Lovat Road, opened it slightly and called, "Hello Mrs Devine, it's only myself! Are you in?"
He knew fine well that she would be in, she was hardly ever out, but it was only good manners to ask.
"Come away in John, you must have heard the kettle going on!"

 The tea was made, the scones were brought through, and a wee pot of homemade gooseberry jam completed the tasty *strupag (a wee cup of tea – a tasty repast)*.

"That's a fine sight for any man, Mrs Devine," Bookem said as he eyed the scones and jam.

"Now, remember, it's *Lizzie*, not Mrs Devine! I can't be doing with all that folderol."

"Alright Lizzie, I'll remember that," Bookem replied with a smile. He never presumed to call someone by their first name without their permission, it was a sign of respect, but sure, is it not just good manners?

"Now John, what do I owe the pleasure of having you this evening?"

"Well, there has been a number of reports of the 'Whisperings' starting up again. The first one or two were heard by two towerists (*tourists*) but I've had three reports from locals too – and I'm not sure what to make of it, Lizzie. What do you think?"

"Whisperings, eh? It's many years since I last heard of such things. I remember there was a spate of them some years ago in Callart Forest.

The strange thing was that the voices got louder as you got nearer the old Church there. The bells would ring in the dead of night, despite the Church not being used for many years, but they haven't been heard for some years now. A strange business, right enough."

"Well, it's funny that you should say that, but the Callart church bells were heard to be ringing just a few nights ago, and again last night, that's what has prompted me to come and see yourself, Mrs Devine, sorry, Lizzie."

"Oh dear, it is a worry to be sure. The bells will be an omen of something to come, and the whisperings will be the souls of those departed, talking, chattering and calling out.
That area is a place where the air is thinner between this world and the next," Lizzie continued. "It is believed to have started when the plague struck down the whole Cameron family who lived there in the early 1600's.

They all died, except the youngest daughter, Mary."

"It is said that her mother is calling her from the other side. Calling her to take her own life and so join with the family in the world beyond.

It was quite common for those with 'the gift' to hear the 'whisperings' through the veil – but it has been many years since they have been heard at Callart – it seems like the chattering, the whispering, is starting again.

Something is afoot, John, something is happening, but I haven't heard what it is. If the whisperers are restless, it doesn't bode well, it doesn't bode well at all," said Mrs Devine with a strained look of foreboding.

Bookem knew her well enough to know that she was very concerned – and that troubled him.

The next morning Bookem took a run down the low road from Kinlochleven to Callart to see if he could see or feel something which might help him see things more clearly.

He parked his Land Rover by Callart Church and walked up the track which led into the woods. He spoke to his wee pal, Rory, but then realised that his wee pal was nowhere to be seen. He retraced his steps and saw Rory sitting by the Land Rover – and even when Bookem called him, he wouldn't budge.
He knew Rory well enough to know that he was sensitive to 'certain things' – so he smiled and opened the passenger's door to the Land Rover, and Rory jumped up onto the seat and curled up.

Bookem walked back to the forest and straight away he felt a distinct chill in the air, even though it was a warm, day.
Then he heard someone call out his name, *John. John,* and he turned and looked around, trying to locate the voice but there was no-one there, at least, not as far as he could see.
The wind was blowing and the leaves rustled as the tree branches began to swish.
If he didn't know better, he would swear that the trees had come to life and were calling,

whispering to each other in hushed tones.
It was an eerie experience – one which he had only felt once before, when he was in the woods at Glenachulish, some time ago.
He would normally put such things down to an overactive imagination, but today, he wasn't so sure.

He took his courage in his hands and called out, "What is it? What's troubling you?"
The wind blew louder, and the branches whirled and swirled with greater intensity.
Bookem felt there was a restless, agitated, angry atmosphere blowing in the wind. Yes, that was it, it was like the trees were angry.
Bookem began to doubt his sanity as he could hear voices blowing through the wind.
He strained his ears – what were they saying? What was going on? What was happening? Was he dreaming all of this, or was it real?
He felt he was caught in some kind of extraordinary hallucination. Just then, the wind stopped, the branches came to rest and there was an eerie silence… and to Bookem's great

surprise, a pure white fawn appeared from behind a holly bush and walked towards him. Bookem froze.

He had experienced many strange things in his years in the Highlands and Islands, things he couldn't explain, but this was beyond all reason.

How could the trees become angry? How could the branches possibly speak? It was crazy, but there it was – he could see it, hear it and most certainly feel it for himself.

The young deer walked right up to Bookem, and he held out his hand and touched the fawn's head. It was completely undaunted.

Bookem stroked its head and ears and said gently, "What is it? What's troubling you?"

The young deer took hold of Bookem's cuff and tugged at it, pulling him to follow.

It was all so surreal, but he had come this far, so he decided to follow the fawn – but where would it take him? Only the good Lord knew that.

Bookem said a short prayer asking for God's protection and safekeeping, then he stood and walked forward as the fawn led the way.

After a few minutes, the fawn stopped and scraped at the ground.
Bookem stepped forward and on clearing away the earth, leaves and branches, he saw a large Ballachulish slate with a skull and crossbones (ancient *symbols of immortality*) etched upon it. It was a *very* old grave.
He thought he knew these woods fairly well, but he had never seen or heard about a grave being hereabouts.
The inscription on the slate was, *'Annie Campbell, 'Witch of Call-ort was burned to death here on 7th November 1252 .'*

Annie Campbell had been a witch who had the 'evil eye,' it was said, and was much feared for her ability to cast spells and call up evil spirits. Although she had been burned at the stake, there were reports that she was seen on a number of occasions after her 'death.'

The strange thing was, that the church bell had rung on the night before her death – although there was no-one in the church at the time.

Over the years, it has rung of its own accord – and always on the eve of a death within the parish bounds.

It is an eerie sound, to hear the soulful toll of a solitary bell in the dark, foretelling a death. Who would it be…?

Bookem knew well of Annie Campbell's reputation, and his own Island upbringing had taught him not to treat such things lightly.

He felt a dark foreboding around him and the whispering voices were growing louder again, so he decided to leave, after all, he thought, he could always come back at a later date.

He glanced around and took in the surroundings so he could find the place again – then walked slowly away.

The voices were getting so loud that he had to put his hands over his ears as he hurried out of the woods.

The very moment that he stepped out of the dark shadows of the trees, there was a sudden silence. Bookem had never experienced anything like it before.

He wasn't a man to be easily scared, but his hands were shaking as he opened the driver's door of his Land Rover and climbed in.
His faithful dog, Rory, who had been anxiously waiting for him, jumped up onto his lap and licked his pale face.
He sat there for a good few minutes as he composed himself before setting off back up the road to Kinlochleven and Lizzie Devine's house.
Maybe *she* could make some sense of all this. If anyone could, it would be her.

"Och. It's yourself John, come away in." Lizzie was always pleased to see her favourite Polisman.
He told Lizzie about all he had seen, heard and felt in Callart Woods. "Mo Chreach-sa thàinig! *(Oh my goodness!)* quite an ordeal for you."

"I knew that the good Lord was with me, but it was unsettling never-the-less. But what do you think it all means, Lizzie?"

"Well, since you last spoke to me, I've been doing some searching of my own, and it seems that something is brewing. I haven't found out exactly what it is yet, but it's something to do with the Witch of Callart, Annie Campbell, said to be descended from Corrag, the Witch of Glencoe.

The whisperers are anxious and there is much unrest among them. I have heard your name being mentioned a few times. You must be careful John, there's a darkness in it."

Bookem was troubled by Lizzie Devine's remarks, and tried to make light of it by saying, "Well, don't worry, I'll be alright, my trusty Rory will protect me!"
"It's no matter for the jokes, John, you *must* be careful!"
"Aye, you are right, of course, Lizzie."

He paused and scratched his head - "But what do we do now?"

"Well, John, as I see it, there are two options – we either wait and see what happens, or we follow the trail and see where it leads us. What do you think yourself?"

But before he could answer, a thought jumped into Lizzie's mind and she said – "John, what is today's date?"
"Um, I'm not sure. Let me see.. Sunday was the 31st of October. Today is Friday so, it must be…" he counted on his fingers… "So, today is the 5th, aye, the 5th of November.
"So, this coming Sunday must be the 7th of November?"
"That's right Lizzie, what are you thinking?"
"I remember reading somewhere that Annie Campbell vanished on the 7th November 1252. It was 7pm when she was last seen by Lachie MacDonald the gamekeeper."
John was beginning to see what Lizzie was saying.

"So, Sunday will be the 7th of November 1952, exactly 700 years since her disappearance."
"Aye John, that's *exactly* what I am thinking. The 7th day, at 7pm, 700 years later. That's a lot of 7's! – coincidence? I don't believe in coincidences John, and I have a feeling that something is going to happen quite soon. My best guess is on Sunday, 7th quite possibly at 7 o'clock in the evening, at the Callart church!"

"By jove Lizzie, I think you've hit the nail on the head. We must find out what it is…"
"Yes John, and you must stop it!" Lizzie Devine interrupted.
"Me!" John wasn't so sure about that.
"Aye John, *you!*"
"Mo chrach-sa thàinig!" *(Mo chraachsa hanik, Oh, my goodness!),* John said as he realised the enormity of what lay ahead, whatever that may be.
It was now Friday evening – they had until 7pm on Sunday to come up with a viable plan!

Bookem remembered a similar situation when he was the Polis-man on the little Island of Rhua.

Dark forces had been at work there, and it had been the 'Meenister,' the Reverend Colin Campbell and his Elders, who had saved the day *(see my 'Even More Tales of a Highland Minister,' Book 3, Chapter 10, The 'Witches' Cat.')*

"I have an idea Lizzie, I'll be back in the morning to let you know how I get on."

"Alright John, be sure and keep yourself safe."

"I will," replied John. "And if you can find out more of what is going on, that would be a great help. See you in the. Morning."

With that, he left Lizzie and hurried back to the Police Station to put his plan together.

When he got in, he fed his wee pal Rory and poured himself a decent sized dram, just to help his concentration.

He licked the end of his pencil and stared at his notebook. Where to start?

After a couple of minutes, he wrote down a few notes, scratched his head and felt he was on the right track. The dram had helped, so much so that he thought it best to have another.

Half an hour later, he had the outline of a plan, well, it was more like a skeleton of an outline of a sort of rough plan.
He knew what he had to do – it was just a matter of putting it into practice on the night – and that wouldn't be quite so straightforward.
But, first things first. He knew that if his plan was to succeed, he would need help – and time was of the essence.
He had written down the names of a few people that he knew he could depend on, but he had to talk to them first.

Himself and Rory jumped into his Land Rover and headed out to make a few house calls.
By the time he got home it was late, and he burned the midnight oil fine tuning his final plan.

The next morning, Saturday, he visited Lizzie Devine to update her on his plan.

"What do you think, Lizzie?" He was eager to hear what his good friend thought of his proposal.

Lizzie read it slowly, then went over it again.
"It sounds like a good plan John, but dangerous too! You will have to be on your guard, or who knows what fate might befall you. By all accounts, Annie Campbell was a cruel, cunning, ruthless witch, capable of calling up the most foul and wicked forces."

They talked it through for the next hour or so, ironing out a few details here and there until they were satisfied with a final plan.

"I'm still not completely happy John, but it will work if the good Lord is with us."
"Aye Lizzie, you can be sure that He *will* be."
"Then we need have no fear." Lizzie Devine replied.
John agreed but couldn't help being apprehensive of what might lie ahead.

Bookem had arranged that they should all meet outside the old Callart church at 6.30 the following evening, that being Sunday the 7th of November 1952, exactly 700 years since the dark witch, Annie Campbell had been burned at the stake, or so it was thought.

Bookem attended Church as usual that morning and was greatly encouraged by the Sermon which was taken from Psalm 37 at verse 5 which says, *'Commit your ways to the LORD, trust in Him and He will bring it to pass.'*

He knew that whatever happened at Callart that evening, his faithful God would be with him and all would be well.

He had called upon God to sustain him in the most trying times of his life – and God had not forsaken him. And so, he knew that God would not desert him that very night, when he needed help the most.

Feeling much more confident, Bookem spent Sunday afternoon fine tuning his plan.

He left the Police station for Callart Church at

6 o'clock that evening and felt fully prepared for whatever evil forces may be sent to frustrate him.

As he drove along the twisty road, he repeated words from the Old Testament – *'Those who trust in the Lord, will find their strength renewed.'* (Isaiah 40 verse 31).

By the time he arrived, he felt invincible – no witch was going to get the better of *him*, he had God on his side!

It was dark when he arrived at Callart Church. The first thing he noticed was a large black Hearse parked in the small Car park. He knew it belonged to one of the Free church elders, John Miller and wondered if that was an omen of things to come, he hoped not.

A small group of chosen friends met him. There was the Free Church Minister, Rev. Colin McAulay, the Episcopalian Priest Rev. Ian Russell and his own Minister, Rev. Bill Fleming, along with three Elders from each of the churches, numbering 12 in all, the same number as there had been Disciples.

Bookem was greeted with a cry of – "Hello, it's yourself!" by his friend, the Reverend Colin of the Free Church.

"Aye, it is that! Are you ready for the fray, Colin?" Bookem replied.
"As ready as I'll ever be, John." Reverend McAulay replied.
"Okay, gather round and let's go over the plan one last time," Bookem said.
Before discussing tactics, the group bowed their heads as Reverend McAulay put up a prayer, asking for God's strength and protection against evil forces and whatever may confront them, that fateful night – and they all said 'Amen.'
Bookem outlined their responsibilities and looked at each one of them, they nodded in turn.
"Well, time marches on, we had better get going – and may the Good Lord be with us.
Let's go!"

As they walked through the woods, the soft whisperings of many voices slowly got louder. They looked at each other and huddled closer, looking this way and that, expecting some awful apparition to leap out at them at any moment.

Bookem sensed their uneasiness and said, "Stay strong, best foot forward," and he started to sing the 23rd Psalm – "*The Lord is my shepherd, I shall not want…*" and they all lifted up their heads and joined in.
The whisperings were getting louder with each minute, motivating the courageous little band to raise their voices even more.
Bookem led the way, holding up a crudely fashioned Cross made of hazel wood (*known for its qualities of giving protection from evil*).

As they came to a clearing, Bookem recognised it as the site where he had seen the large Ballachulish slate with 'Annie Campbell, 'Witch of Call-ort' etched upon it, along with a number of mystic symbols which he didn't recognise.

"This is it!" Bookem called out. The small procession stopped, and they looked around with a mixture of both fear and intrigue.
They all knew the tales of Annie Campbell, they had heard them at their grandmother's knee.

Suddenly, the heavens opened, and the rain came on and grew ever heavier by the minute. Within just a few minutes they were all soaked to the skin, but their spirits were not dampened.
Their Tilly Lamps flickered and went out, and they stood in darkness, except for a narrow shaft of moonlight which shone down through the trees, directly onto the grave like the beam of a searchlight.
There were a few moments of silence – then, suddenly, a flash of lightning crashed through the forest, making everyone jump.
It lit up the clearing and they saw a number of shadowy figures moving around in the bushes. Their hearts were beating fifteen to the dozen.

"Stand Firm!" Bookem shouted, "Remember the Scriptures tell us ~ *"Be strong and courageous. Do not be afraid, do not be discouraged, for the Lord your God is with you." (Joshua 1: 9).*

With renewed vigour, the Elders formed a circle around the grave - Bookem and the three Ministers stood at each of the four corners of the grave.

The Episcopal Priest put up a prayer, laid down a Palm leaf *(A symbol of victory over spiritual enemies)* and swung a Censer three by three times over the grave. The aroma of the incense was both pungent and powerful.

The thunder got louder, and the rain became more torrential than anyone had ever seen before - *and that is saying something in the Highlands!*

A fierce wind got up, causing an eerie howling noise which sent a shiver of fear up the spine of all present.

"Oh my goodness, God save us!" one of the Elders shouted.

Bookem saw their fear and called out, *"Our Father, who art in Heaven, hallowed be thy name..."* and everyone joined in with the Lord's Prayer. *"Thy kingdom come, thy will be done on earth as it is in Heaven, give us this day our daily bread and forgive us our debts as we forgive our debtors – Lead us not into temptation – but deliver us from evil..."* and as they called out those last heartfelt words, <u>*'deliver us from evil,'*</u> the rain stopped as quickly as it had started. They looked at each other, lost for words.

But then, they heard the most beautiful choir singing – and a warm, bright glow encompassed them.

They stood in silence, feeling the warmth, sensing that they were in the presence of a higher power. Then there was silence.

"Praise God!" said Reverend Fleming, and he started to clap.

The others, some moved to tears, joined in the applause which grew and grew until there was a feeling of great triumph and thanksgiving for God's amazing power over evil.

"Well John," said the Free Church Minister, "your plan certainly worked, well done!" and patted Bookem on the back.

"It wasn't me, it was God that was in it, I just put it all in His holy hands and he did the rest."

"Aye, John, you're some man!" one of the Elders said.

"Och, away with you," John said, turning a bright shade of red.

They were in high spirits as they walked back to the car park.

One of the Free Church Elders, (who was the local Undertaker) opened up the back of his Hearse and handed a glass to each Elder and poured them each a bumper Dram and proposed a toast ~ "To our Lord and Saviour – and Constable Malcolm!"

Everyone repeated the words of the toast and gave a cheer.

Bookem blushed and said, "Och, there's no need for that, boys," with his usual air of humility.

He left Callart and went straight up to Lizzie Devine's home in Kinlochleven.

He talked her through how things had gone and was keen to say that it wasn't himself that had overcome the evil forces.

"Aye John, it's modest that you are!" Lizzie said to him. "You certainly had a hand in it!"

"We all played our part, Lizzie. Have you heard any more whisperings?"

"It's a funny you should ask that. There was a frenzy of chatter up until about 7.30 tonight – and then it stopped abruptly, and it has been silent since. "

John knew that was the same time as they were praying for deliverance.

A couple of months later, on January 1st, John decided to pay a visit to Callart and take a walk through the woods there.

His trusty wee dog, Rory, happily ran beside him as he walked to the site where Annie Cambell's grave had been, but to his amazement, there was no grave, no Ballachulish slate, it was as if it had never been there.

Bookem looked around and felt a whole new atmosphere from his first visit there.

It was bright, warm, and the birds were singing their merry songs.

Did the whole business of that dark night in November *really* take place?
Had it all been a dream?
He sat on a fallen tree trunk, and his mind went back to that fateful night.
As he pondered all that had happened on November 7th, something caught his attention out of the corner of his eye, a small white deer was looking at him through a holly bush.
As he took a closer look, he was sure it was the very same white fawn that had led him to the site of Annie Campbell's grave.

As he watched, the fawn walked slowly out of the bushes and cautiously approached him.
Bookem held his hand out and stroked the fawn's head as it drew closer, it was a surreal moment.
After a few minutes, the fawn walked slowly away and disappeared into the undergrowth.

Was it, in some way, thanking Bookem for his part in banishing evil forces from the woods?

It was a special moment for this wily old Policeman – and it reinforced his belief that God had been with them on that dark, scary night in November as they overcame the dark forces of evil.

"Aye," he said to himself, "God is good, right enough," and his wee Pal, Rory, jumped up and licked his face.

Bookem closed his eyes and said, "Thank you, Lord" – and they both walked back to the Land Rover and made their way back to the Police Station for a cup of tea and a treat for Rory – after stopping in the Ferryman's Bar at Ballachulish Ferry for a 'wee sensation,' purely for medicinal purposes, of course.

*

P.S: I remember one dark night, when I was in my teens, my girlfriend and I were walking back from Ballachulish to her home in Glencoe when we heard the Callart Church bell ringing from across the other side of Loch Leven.

It was a spine-chilling, mournful sound that sent shivers down our spines.

We knew the tales and heard the stories about the Callart Church bell, but to hear it for ourselves was a different matter.

We quickened our pace until we reached the 'bright lights' of the Glencoe hotel aka 'The Grotto' (there were no street- lights along that stretch of road at that time).

The only good thing to come out of it was – as we hurried along the dark road between Ballachulish and Glencoe - she squeezed my hand tighter and snuggled into my side.

Clouds and silver linings.

'The Curious Case of The Vanishing Ferryman'

5.

It was a cold, damp January day in Ballachulish. The dark clouds were gathering, and the wind was blowing the snow into a frenzy.

Donnie MacDougall, otherwise known as 'Bumper,' and Lachie McColl were just beginning their morning shift on the Ballachulish Ferry.
Bumper was prepared for the wintery weather, he had a hot water bottle in his inside pocket.
Well, I say 'hot water bottle', actually it was a half bottle of Whisky, but the effect is just the same.
"Aye, it's great for keeping out the cold," he would say to anyone who would care to ask why.
 Bumper was known for 'taking a dram,' indeed, it was quite a pastime of his.

"Some folks like the gardening," he would say, "And others enjoy the fishing, but I neffer saw the satisfaction in any of that. You can't beat a good dram of the Uisge to relax you after a hard day."

"*Aye,*" thought Lachie, "*I've seen him as 'relaxed as a newt' on many occasions.*"

"Not only that," Bumper continued, "think of all those good, hard working, family men who work in the Distilleries, am I not keeping them in a job so they can put food in the mouths of their wee ones? Aye there would be bairns in Islay starving in their beds, I couldn't have that on my conscience."

Bumper felt justly proud of his sacrifice as he lit up another 'roll up' and fired up the engine. "Aye, you're a local hero right enough, Bumper, "replied Lachie. "It's the medal you should be getting."

"Och, away with you Lachie, you know me, I don't like any fuss, it's the humility that's in me."

Lachie smiled, "Aye, just that Bumper, just that."

Lachie was Bumper's rope man - the one who jumped off the boat and tied a rope to one of the rusty iron rings which were dotted along both sides of the jetty. Not for the faint hearted!

Every skipper had his own rope man, but Lachie was held in high esteem among the Ferrymen as he had the record for falling in more times than anyone else since the Ferry first began!
"It's my sense of balance that causes me to fall over, it's a curse on me," he would say in his defence. That, of course, may well be true, but a much more likely explanation could be the contents of the hip flask that he carried with him wherever he went.
"It has the sentimental signification to me. My father carried it with him in the trenches, and the dent on the side is where a German bullet struck, and it saved his life. I'm keeping it on me for the emergencies."
But the other Ferrymen are convinced that the dent was made thon time he fell off the Ferry

and struck the edge of the jetty as he went over the side.

"The white horses are fair getting up," Bumper said as the waves caused the wee boat to rise and fall on its way over to the Loch Leven Hotel side of the narrow crossing.

*

Over the years, all manner of transportation has crossed over on the Ferry.

In olden days, Cattle Drovers with their cattle on the way to markets further south, to 'Onion Johnnies' with their onions tied onto the handlebars on their pushbikes, have crossed these narrow waters.

In more modern times, cars, caravans, push bikes, hikers and motorbikes have crossed, heading North to Fort William or places further North, or South to Oban, Glasgow and beyond.

A few years back, a traditional, brightly coloured, wooden Travellers' Caravan pulled by a large black horse, was transported to the North side on their way to a 'Tinkers Wedding' on the Black Isle.

As you might imagine, much fun was had trying to get the horse onto the Ferry boat on a wet and windy day!

But today looked like being the same as any other day – rain with the forecast of more rain, but neither Bumper nor Lachie could possibly have known what was about to unfold, and perhaps that was just as well.

It was Hogmanay, well, I say Hogmanay, it was January the 11th, the day before the *'Old New Year'* which was still observed by many in the Highlands on the 12th.
Bumper had already celebrated the New Year on the 1st January along with the rest of Scotland, but he believed in keeping up the 'old traditions' and so he celebrated both Hogmanays. It has been known for him to go missing for a week or so during this 'suspicious occasion' as he liked to call it.
He had cousins in just about every other croft in Glenachulish – and felt obliged to visit each one.

"If I was to miss anyone in my visitations, they would be much offended, and it would bring them the most awful bad luck, and I wouldn't want to be doing that!"

Every year he went missing for a week or so - and every year he emerged looking like "death warmed up," as his long suffering wife, Mairead (Margaret), said.

Two years ago, his excuse was - "It was a bad whisky that thon incomer gave me, what's wrong with a good Highland Malt anyway!?"

Last year, his defence was – "It was thon pie that old Mrs McCallum gave me, I tried to feed it to the dog when she was out in the kitchen pouring another dram, but even the wee dog wouldn't touch it!"

However, this year was different. It had been nearly 3 weeks since Hogmanay, and there was still no sign of Bumper.

His beloved Mairead didn't seem too worried, "He's like the bad penny," she said, "He'll turn up before too long. You mark my words…."

But he didn't – turn up, that is.

The weeks passed, and still, there was no sign of Bumper. Mairead had to admit that it wasn't like him.

"I have a bad feeling about this – it goes against the grain, but there's nothing else for it but to call in Constable Bookem," Mairead said.

"Och, he'll have us all booked for wasting Polis time," Mairead's sister Peggy remarked with a certain amount of personal experience.
"Do you remember last Christmas when me and you got lifted for shop lifting in Oban?"
"Aye," said Peggy, "Thon was diabolical, thon was! Mind you, they *did* find all those cigarettes and two half bottles in your shopping bag."
"Aye well, that was planted on me by the Polis! They were out to get me after the time they chased me into Woolworth's and I gave them the slip, the buggers!"
"Aye, they are that," Peggy agreed. "And they've long memories too!"

"Aye," was all Mairead could say.
"But if they could help find Bumper, perhaps we should let them look for him," Peggy suggested.
"I suppose you're right Peggy, but hell mend him when I get my hands on him!" Mairead said as she rolled up her sleeves in anticipation.

A search of the Glen was undertaken, and Constable Bookem oversaw the operation.
"Okay lads, search every croft and byre in the glen, he has to be somewhere," Bookem said to the group of volunteers.
"He's probably sleeping off a major hangover somewhere," one of the team remarked.
"Now, there's no need for that, Angus!" Bookem rebuked young Angus Bethune.
"But there's a fair chance you're right, Angus, but we won't know unless we find him, so let's get going!
We'll start with his cousins at the far end of the glen and work our way back down to the village."
And so, the search began.

Two days passed and there was still no sign of Bumper.

"I'll not beat about the bush, Mairead, it's not looking good. I thought we would have found him by now," Bookem admitted.

"Och, he's an awful man, Mr Bookem, always getting up to mischief and has an over-liking for the drams, but I miss him getting under my feet," Mairead said with a tear in her eye.

Bookem was quite touched as he'd never seen the softer side of Mairead McDougall before.

He had only known the coarse, insensitive, loud, critical and abrasive side of her, but he was now seeing her in a completely new light.

Well, until she said, *"Wait 'til I get him home, I'll skin him alive, the no good layabout!"* that was.

It was another 2 days before Bumper was to surface.

As part of the search, Mrs Fraser had visited a number of remote crofts in the glen to inquire if anyone had seen Bumper in the past few weeks.

Most of them said that they had indeed seen him during his annual 'grand tour of the glen,' as he called it, but he had only stayed a few hours and moved on to the next croft, as was his custom.

It wasn't until Mrs Fraser visited the remote croft, 'Moss Cottage,' *(Tigh-còinneach)* that her suspicions were aroused.

The widow, Joan Clarke (*who had recently moved up from the south and was generally seen, by the local ladies, as 'mutton dressed as lamb'*) was very vague as to whether Bumper had visited her in his 'first footing' tour.

Mrs Clarke kept Mrs Fraser at the door but she could see into the house and saw a pile of empty whisky bottles and cans of Lager *(the ones with the pictures of various beauty queens on the back)* lying beside an armchair. Next to the lager cans were a number of Country and Western LP sleeves. Patsy Cline was singing one of her famous songs, "I'm hungry for Love," on the record player.

Yes, suspicious in itself, but it was when she saw what looked like Bumper's 'Captain's cap' on the hat stand by the door, that her suspicions were confirmed.

She made a speedy exit and raced back to report to Bookem.

She went straight to the Police Station in Glencoe and related all that she had seen and heard at Moss Cottage.

"What makes you think Bumper is with this 'lady,' Mrs Fraser?"

"I saw Bumper's cap hanging on the hat stand by the door,"

"But how did you know it was *his* cap?"

"Because it still had the Poppy on the side, it's been there since a week before Remembrance Day in November last year!"

"Aye, that's his bunnet alright, well done Mrs Fraser.

I've had my suspicions about that lady for some time now," Bookem said.

"Yes, she is a shady lady if ever there was one! With her bleach blonde hair and fancy painted fingernails. I'd bet good money those hands have never milked a cow or gutted a 'troot' (a Trout) in her life!" Bookem drew breath and continued, "Well, we'd better get going before it's too late!"

Bookem, two of his Special Constables and his wee dog Rory, jumped into his Land Rover and made their way up to Moss Cottage at speed, time was of the essence!
"There's no time to waste lads," Bookem said as he put his foot down on the accelerator and raced up to 50 miles an hour!
If ever there was a 'man on a mission,' it was Constable Bookem, '*The scourge of the criminal classes*!'

As they pulled up outside Moss Croft, they saw Mrs Clarke looking out of the window. When she saw PC Bookem's Land Rover pull up. She screamed and drew the curtains over.
"Aye, she's fly, that one," said John Angus, (one of the Special Constables).
"Aye, she knows we're on to her, the Hussy!" Bookem replied, keen to get going.

They all jumped out of the Land Rover and Bookem shouted. "You two, surround the house!"

John Angus and Ewan McColl (the other special Constable) looked at each other, and Ewan said, "What, the two of us, surround the house?"

"Aye, get round the back and make sure no-one makes a run for it!" Bookem shouted as he thumped on the front door.

"The game's up! Don't be causing a fracarse, it'll be easier on you in court!" Bookem was in no mood to take prisoners, except for the culprit, Mrs Clark, of course.

"Come out with your hands up," Bookem shouted – *had he been reading too many American 'cop' books?*

The front door opened and Mrs Clarke came out with her hands held up high and sobbing intensely.

"It wasn't me!" she said.

"That's what they all say!" Bookem said, "Come quietly now."

Meanwhile, Bookem's wee dog, Rory, ran into the house – and within a few minutes came running out again.

He ran over to Bookem and nudged his leg.

"He's on to something!" Bookem said and followed Rory into the house and through to the bedroom. Rory sat staring at the wardrobe, whining.

"He's in here, boys! The wee fellow has found Bumper! Good boy!" Rory's tail was wagging excitedly.

As Bookem opened the wardrobe door, Bumper slid out and crumpled onto the bedroom floor, raised his hands and said, "Halleluiah, praise the Lord! I've been saved!"

You are my Saviour, Constable Bookem. That… that, Jezebel kept me prisoner. It's been sheer hell I tell you, sheer hell!…thank you, thank you." he said emotionally.

"Don't thank _me_, thank wee Rory, the best police dog in the Force!" Bookem said proudly.

But, for as pleased as he was, he felt that something wasn't quite right.

He couldn't put his finger on it, but he felt uneasy. Perhaps it was his well tuned sense of 'detectification,' as he called it.

Over the next few days, Mrs Clarke was questioned, however, Bumper said he was 'too traumatised' to make a statement, so Bookem reluctantly had to release her, due to the lack of evidence that any crime had been committed.
"There's something not right in this business, not right at all, at all." He said, scratching his head.

As the weeks went by, Bumper regaled the lads in the Ferry Bar with stories of his 'incarceration' at Mrs Clarke's croft.
"You'll never know how much I suffered, it was sheer hell, I'm fair exhausted," he said with a smile and a wink. "I'll need to take another dram to calm my nerves…"
"Tell us more, Bumper," the 'boys' would say as they nudged each other and set up another dram for their new found hero, Donnie MacDougall, aka Bumper.

A few weeks later, Mrs Clarke came into the Glencoe Police station and told Bookem what *really* happened.

It appeared that during his Hogmanay travels, Bumper had dropped in to wish her a Happy New Year and fallen asleep in the armchair.

Try as she might, she couldn't wake him up, and so she threw a blanket over him and let him sleep it off.

When she went through to the living room the next morning, she found him lying on the floor, with a dram of her best '8 year old Islay Mist Whisky' in his hand, singing along to her Patsy Cline Country and Western L.P's.

Their mutual love of Patsy Cline had brought them closer together, and they fell in love singing, 'Your Cheating Heart', with Bumper doing the harmonies.

She said that he didn't want to go back to Mairead, his wife, but had wanted to stay with her in her cottage up the Glen.

"What could I do? Donald is such a charmer!"

"Are we still talking about Bumper?" Bookem

enquired, thinking that she might have wandered off into another story.

"Oh yes, Mr Bookem, He's such a man of the world. He told me all about the medals he won in the War and how Mr Churchill sent him a personal letter of thanks for all his 'under the cover' work he did on the Ferry, although he can't find the letter now," and she gave a sigh.

"Yes, he has stolen my heart Mr Bookem. Oh, Donald, my Scottish hero!" and she gave another sigh.

"Bumper? A hero? I think there's some mistake, Bumper never got any further than Catterick. He got sent home with his knees."

"Oh yes, he said people would say that. Jealousy is a terrible thing, Mr Bookem."

Once the story had got out, the gossips had a field day.

Bumper's wife, Mairead, was arrested for attempted 'gregarious bodily harm' as she battered Bumper with his own Shinty stick, which he kept behind the front door in case of emergencies.

His 'street cred' rose to near hero status, especially among his pals in the Ferry Bar.

"Aye, thon Bumper, he's some lad right enough!" was the general feeling among the lads.

Indeed, whenever Bumper's name was mentioned, someone always said. "Aye, the Bumper is some lad!"

Maybe, one day, they will put that on his gravestone.

*

P.S. Not that long ago, I was travelling from Oban to visit family in Kinlochleven and I stopped to have a look around Duror and Kentallen Cemetery to see if I could find Bumpers' grave.

After a while of searching, I found it – and sure enough, underneath the moss, engraved on his Headstone, were the words ~

   'Here lies the Bumper
   He was some lad'
    R. I. P.

'The Curious Case of the Mystery at the Blackwater Dam'

6.

The lads of the 'Hill Squad' were (and still are) the men who carried out repair and maintenance work at the Blackwater Dam and the associated pipe track maintenance in the hills above Kinlochleven in Argyll. They go out in all weathers, day and sometimes night, if needed, which wasn't often.

The Dam was built at great cost to life in the early 1900's where many Navvies perished due to hard work, accidents (which were frequent) or the freezing conditions in winter.

The little, remote graveyard there is a poignant reminder of the callous disregard for life, and there are many tales of ghosts being seen, and other strange happenings there.

It certainly has a sombre atmosphere around it. Not a place to hang around after dark, that is for sure!

It was the early hours of the morning of 1st May 1955, when the mournful sound of the factory hooter was heard throughout the small village of Kinlochleven.

It sounded like the mournful sound of a ship's horn sounding in a cold, dark, foggy night.

It gave two short and two long blasts.

Many of the villagers woke with a start, fearing the worst, as it was a call for the men of the hill squad to assemble at the gate of the Aluminium works.

Within 15 minutes the lads of the hill squad gathered at the gates of the factory – all of them were anxious. Being called out at that time of the morning was never going to be good news.

The youngest member of the Squad was a man, a boy really, called Frank Cochrane. He stood shivering in the cold, dark night, wondering what lay ahead for them.

He had only been a member of the Hill Squad for a few weeks, and this callout so early in the morning was something new, something he could well do without.

The fact that the local Policeman's Land Rover was parked beside the main Factory gate didn't go unnoticed.
The tall, street lamp, which illuminated the entrance to the factory, shone an eerie yellow halo around the men as they waited to hear why they had been called out at such an unearthly hour.

Just then, the office door opened and out walked the Factory Manager, Nigel Herrick, Constable Bookem, the local Bobby, and the Hill Squad gaffer, Murdo Munro.

Mr Herrick spoke – "Constable Malcolm informs me that he has received reports of lights being seen up on the hill. We're not sure who or what they are, and the only way we are going to find out is by going up there and finding out for ourselves.
Constable Book… – er, um – Malcolm, will co-ordinate the search, so, let's get cracking – the sooner we get up the hill and find out, the sooner we'll get back to our beds."

Bookem laid out his plan *(which was basically, 'let's go boys and see what we can find up there')* and asked if there were any questions.

Everyone shook their heads, so he said, "Okay lads, let's go!"

Johnny Nope fired up the Land Rover, the boys jumped in the back, and off they went, following Bookem up the pipe-track and on up to the pumping station at the top, a.k.a. the Penstock.

Old Lachie Grant was not happy. "Aye, lights on the hills at night is a bad omen," he said ominously.

"The last time it happened was between the wars – and two of our squad were lost and never seen or heard of since. Aye, lights on the hills at night is a bad omen."

"Och, gonnie no' talk rubbish? Away and bile yer heid," said wee Jimmy.

No one knew his real name, but as he was from Glasgow, and he was quite short, everyone called him 'Wee Jimmy' *(as in 'see you, Jimmy!')*.

Most of the boys in the Hill Squad were, or had been, either shepherds on the Mamore Estate, members of the Glencoe Mountain Rescue Team or locals who knew the hills like the back of their hands.

They scanned the hills, and before long they saw the lights that had been reported.

"There they are!" said Jock Anderson, pointing across the hill.

"It looks like they're coming from the direction of the Dam," young Frank said.

"Aye, I think you're right, let's crack on!" Bookem was eager to find out what this was all about.

The darkness was slowly changing into a misty, early morning light.

As they approached the Dam, they passed the 'Navvies Cemetery.'

It was a sorry sight to see the tumbled down headstones and the little mounds with no name or stone to identify the poor soul that lay interred there and forgotten.

The lights seemed to be hovering above the graveyard, giving an eerie glow.
"Stop! Stop!" one of the boys shouted, "Look!" and he pointed to the graveyard.
"Can you see it?" he said excitedly.
Suddenly, they all saw it – the body of a man lying full length on top of one of the graves.
"There, didn't I tell you, lights on the hills at night is a bad omen," Lachie said again.
"Gonnie give it a rest Lachie?" wee Jimmy said as he looked around, unsure of what might happen next.
The rest of the boys were on edge too, after all, it isn't every day you see a dead body with eerie lights hovering over it, in an old disused cemetery.

Bookem took control of the situation saying, "Okay boys, don't panic, stay calm, now."
They looked at each other, they were far from panicking, in fact they were speechless, unsure of just what it was they were witnessing.

Lachie was shaking his head, saying, "Ò mo

chreach! Ò mo chreach, Tha a' diabhail ann! "
(Oh my God, O my God, it's the Devil that's in it!).

Jimmy jumped up and said, "I'm gonnie split his lip if he disnae shut his geggie! I'm gonnie, I'm gonnie!"
"Now, now, Jimmy, take it easy. We're all in this together, so let's not fall out," Bookem said. "I'll go over and see if he's still alive," and he jumped out of the Land Rover and made his way over to the little cemetery, followed by the others.
Johnny Nope remarked, "He was a poor soul, whoever he was."
His hands were callused, he wore a rag for a neckerchief, and his boots were badly worn through at the toe, which revealed that he was not wearing socks.
"He looks just like….." and they all seemed to be thinking the same thing. "He looks like a Navvy." Jock Anderson said.
"You don't think…?"
"Aye that's what I am thinking too," said Bookem.

"But, but, I mean how could it *be*?" Murdo the gaffer said, shaking his head.

"How could it be *what*?..." Frank was lost and had no idea what the others were talking about.

"We're thinking that perhaps... perhaps he is a Navvy from the days they built the dam!" Murdo said hesitantly.

They all knew it was impossible... but there he was, lying on top of a grave, looking for all the world like he had laid down to sleep many years ago and just hadn't woken up, but of course that wasn't possible – was it?...

Wee Jimmy shook his head and said, "You teuchters, *(Choochters, a derogatory term for someone from the Highlands)*, you're full of stories about ghosties, and Whigmaleeries, gonnie get a grip o' yersel's!

"That's enough Jimmy!" Bookem said sternly. "Have we not got enough to think about without casting 'asperations' at each other!"

Bookem went forward and felt the man's wrist to see if there was a pulse.

"No pulse, and he is very cold, he's been here for a long time, I'd say."
Jock Anderson said hesitantly, "When you say, 'a long time,' do you mean... a _long_ time?...."
"Aye, Jock, longer than is plausible. I don't like this," said Bookem, "I don't like this at all, at all!"

Lachie Grant was shaking his head as he said, "Don't say I didn't warn you!
Did I not say, 'Lights on the hills at night is a bad omen'?"
Jimmy took a dive at Lachie, "Right, I warned ye, ya heider!" *(head case)*.
Big Johnny Nope managed to grab Jimmy's jacket collar and haul him back, saying, "Okay Jimmy, cool it! We're all on edge, but falling out isn't going to help anyone."
"Aye, well," said Jimmy, relieved that he didn't have to put his words into actions. Lachie was a little older than him but still looked fit for all that.
Little did he know that Lachie had been one of the hardy men who had been 'Lovat Scouts' at

the end of WW 1 and WW2 *(See Footnote below).*
Bookem was kneeling beside the Navvy, trying to make sense of it all. *"Some thing, some force, has led us here for a reason, but what, and why?"* He thought to himself.

Just at that, a crash of thunder shattered the silence, and a blinding flash of lightning lit up the sky – and the heavens opened.

"Oh Jesus, Joseph and holy Mary!" Jock Anderson shouted loudly. *Which was odd as he wasn't a religious man.*

They ran for shelter and dived into the Land Rover.

The rain was bouncing off the roof so noisily that it sounded like hailstones bouncing off a corrugated-iron bothy.

They were all on edge, wondering what on earth – or *in heaven* – was going on, it was a strange business, right enough.

After a few minutes, Bookem broke the awkward silence.

"Well, boys, what do you make of all this? It's a fair conundrum, to be sure."

Jimmy looked at Lachie, just waiting for him to say something about ghosts or fairies, but Lachie remained silent.

He, like most of the others, had been brought up in the Highlands and had a healthy respect for such things.

"Look outside!" young Frank Cochrane said anxiously.

An eerie, swirling mist had come down and nothing could be seen outside, except for a thick white veil that surrounded them.

He thought it must be what it's like to be sitting inside a cloud.

"Oh mercy! That's us in Heaven now!" Lachie said, looking fearfully through the windscreen.

Bookem could see the anxiety in all their faces.

"Now Lachie, let's just stay calm. If we're in Heaven, then we are nearer to the good Lord." Bookem said. He was fearful too but tried not to show it.

'A calm leader is a good leader, I always say.' He said to himself.

The 'boys' were all for heading home but Bookem was having none of it.
"We came here to find out what in Jehova's name is going on, and by golly we're going to get to the bottom of this."
Bookem could quite easily have gone back to bed, but his sense of duty compelled him to press on and investigate this curious case.

"Right, lads, has anyone got any ideas what the devil is going on here? Lachie, you have the gift, can you shed any light?" Bookem asked.
"Ah well, it's not that easy, you can't just switch it on and off like the Oban Christmas lights, you know!"
"Aye, but can you sense something, *anything* that might help us to make sense of it?" Johny Nope asked.
"Well, all I can say is that I am getting a fearful sense of sorrow. Yes, pain and sorrow. I'll have to go outside to be able to *feel* the atmosphere

and understand where the pain is coming from."

As he went to open the door, Bookem said, "Be careful Lachie, we don't know what these forces are or how dangerous they are. If you're not back in 10 minutes, I'm coming out to get you!"

With that, Lachie climbed out of the Land Rover and walked into the mist.

"Aye, it's brave that he is," said Bookem – and they all nodded in agreement, even wee Jimmy. There was total silence for the next 10 minutes or so.

"Well, I'm going out to see if he is okay. I don't like the feeling I'm getting," Bookem said.

"Aye, neither do I," said Johnny Nope, climbing out of his seat, "I'm coming with you, John."

"Me too…". "And me…". "I'm coming too" and so it was agreed that they would all go, after all were they not friends? And looking out for each other is what friends do.

Bookem was proud of them.

"Okay boys, keep close together, and no sudden movements. Let's go!" and they climbed out of the Land Rover.

"Stay close now, our lives may depend on it!"

"I'm not holding Jimmy's hand!" said Jock Anderson, trying to lighten the mood.

As they slowly walked forward, none of them was quite sure which direction they were going in, the mist was so thick.

"I can see a light!" Jimmy shouted, over there!"

"I see it," Bookem called out. "This way, boys."

As they drew closer to the graveyard, they could make out a figure sitting by a gravestone. It was Lachie.

"Are you alright Lachie?" Bookem shouted, but there was no reply.

As they drew nearer, they could hear Lachie talking as if he were in a conversation, but there was no-one else there – or if there was, they weren't visible.

Bookem crept closer and sat down beside Lachie, not saying a word, just listening.

The one-way conversation went on for another 5 minutes or so. It was like nothing Bookem had ever witnessed before.

Then, without any warning, tears began to run down Lachie's face. Bookem put his arm around him saying, "Don't you be worrying Lachie, my friend, the Good Lord is watching over you and we are all here for you."
As soon as Bookem had said the words, "The Good Lord," the mist (*and the mood*) lifted and within a few moments, the sun came out and it was bright and warm.

Lachie came out of his dwam *(day – dream)* and blinked, rubbing his eyes as he looked around. "When did you all get here?" he asked.
"We've been here for a while Lachie, how are you feeling? Who were you talking to just now?" Bookem asked.
Lachie sat for a minute or two, as if trying to sort things out in his head, and then said, "It was Pádraig Kelly *(pronounced PAW-drig Kelly)*. He worked here on the building of the Dam."

The other lads looked at each other, *after all that was over 40 years ago!*

"And what was he saying to you, Lachie?"
"He said that he wanted me to know just what happened when he was sacked and never seen again."
"Go on." Bookem urged.

"It was the middle of a cold, harsh winter. Cold enough to freeze the devil himself. A young boy, Michael O'Neil, was unwell and frozen to the bone, yet the Gaffer told him to stop slacking and get back to his work. Young Michael wasn't able to stand up and the Gaffer, a cruel man from Glasgow, kicked him hard and the lad had fallen down into the snow.
Pádraig was incensed and hit the Gaffer, who cursed him and told him to pack up his stuff and leave the site immediately.

Young Michael was Pádraig's sister's boy and they had come over from Donegal together to 'get a start' (find work).

They had walked up from Glasgow and 'got a start,' working on the building of the Dam months before. It was hard, gruelling, unrelenting graft.

The Gaffer told Pádraig to '*take this useless boy,*' away with him.

Other Navvies urged the Gaffer to allow them to stay until the weather was better, but he insisted that they leave the site at once.

Pádraig hit him again, and he and the boy walked off into the blizzard – and they were never seen again.

"I knew the story, my father told me of it." Lachie recalled. "But no-one knew what happened to them. No remains were ever found."

"Was that the man we found lying on the grave?" Bookem asked.

"Aye. It was on the 1st of May 1905, 50 years this very day, that they walked into a blizzard.

No-one knew what happened to them, and Pádraig couldn't rest in peace without telling his story.

He said to me, "Now I can pass on to meet my Maker in peace."

"Did he tell you what happened to the two of them?" Bookem asked.

"He did. He said that they followed the path over the hill, as best they could, hoping to make the Kings House and take refuge there.

But they strayed off the path somewhere near the Devil's Staircase, and the boy had slipped and fallen down a steep ravine.

Pádraig had climbed down, hoping to save young Michael but he had twisted his ankle and couldn't walk – and they both perished in the freezing conditions, never to be discovered.

As they all looked down at the grave, there was no body, no lights – just a mound of earth, overgrown and long forgotten – well, forgotten no more.

They drove back down the hill in silence – and when they were asked what they found, they agreed to say ~ "Och it was nothing – it must have been a trick of the light."

But each of them knew the truth – a truth, a secret, that was to bind them together as lifelong friends.

Later ~

They sat in the Canteen Bar and talked over everything they had seen and heard – and resolved to go and find the place, the ravine, where the two hardy Navvies drew their last breath, and erect a small cross in their memory. It was a few weeks later that they walked up the hill in search of the exact location.

As they searched, they came across a ravine, looking down they saw a small cluster of rocks. They agreed that it was the most likely place where the two had ended their days, so they climbed down and erected a small cross made of branches from a Rowan Tree which had sprung up there, among the rocks.

(In Celtic lore, the Rowan tree is believed to have protective powers against evil spirits, witchcraft, and misfortune.)

Even now, if you know where to look, you will see that small cross among the rocks, below a ravine along what is now 'The West Highland Way.'

Hundreds of walkers pass by it every year, completely unaware of the story of the incident at the Blackwater Dam, and the sad fate of those two Irish lads.

There have been stories of walkers hearing voices calling out in that area, but it couldn't possibly be the two Irish Navvies – could it?

*

FOOTNOTE ~*The 'Lovat Scouts' were formed as a Regiment in January 1900 for Service on the Second Boer War by Simon Fraser, 14th Lord Lovat, Chief of Clan Fraser as 'Lovat Scouts.'*

The men were initially recruited from Gamekeepers, Shepherds and men who could live and survive in the hills in all weathers. They undertook clandestine missions behind enemy lines and were renowned for their stealth, resilience and bravery.
Other fields of Combat included, South Africa 1900–02; Gallipoli 1915; Egypt 1915–16; Macedonia 1916–18; France and Flanders 1916–18).

*They wore Hunting Fraser Kilts and their Regimental Cap badge during WW1 and WW2 was the Clan Fraser Crest bearing the words 'Je Suis Prest', which means – 'I am ready.'
Hardy lads.*

'The Curious Case of the Green Lady of Mamore'

7.

The bright winter sun was shining over the pretty little village of Kinlochleven in Argyll, it was like a jewel glistening among the hills which surrounded it.

On the North side, high above the village, stands the impressive Mamore Lodge, (aka Bibby's Lodge) built in 1905 for the wealthy Shipping Magnate, Captain Frank Bibby.

Over the years, there have been a number of sightings of a Lady dressed in green walking the corridors of this imposing Mansion.

Many of the sightings were after a dram or two had been taken, but one 'appearance' stands out among the others and cannot be so easily explained.

It was snowing heavily, and the twinkling lights of Kinlochleven below were barely visible as the mist rolled across the hills.

The night was getting blacker by the minute – and on top of that, the snow was getting heavier.

Not that the residents of Mamore Lodge had noticed.

A party of servicemen were on leave from the 'Front line' in North Africa. The Regiment had suffered many losses and they had been returned to Barracks in Inverness for a well deserved spell of leave.

They were staying at Mamore Lodge for the Hogmanay celebrations, a large log fire was blazing, and a few sociable drams had been taken.

"Another round over here, barman," one of the revellers called – and a cheer went up from the others at the table.

The barman was simply known as 'McKillop.' No one knew what his first name was, presumably he had one, but he seemed happy enough to be known only by his surname.

I would like to say that 'he was happy in his work,' but he was known for his dour manner and dislike of visitors, especially tourists.

He tolerated the guests and was openly rude to anyone who didn't order a 'proper drink.'

On one occasion, a group of hillwalkers came into the lounge and ordered 3 lemonades and a half pint of shandy, at which McKillop exploded saying, "Shandy!? Bloody Shandy!? Take a proper drink man!" and he served the man a pint of Heavy and a half pint of Lager for each of the ladies.

On another occasion, he berated two poor tourists who had the audacity to order two lemonades and a packet of crisps – to which he answered, "Lemonade and a packet of crisps!? What do you think this is, a bloody sweetie shop!"

McKillop nodded to the group of servicemen in response to their order. These were his kind of customers.

He poured six whiskies and carried them over to their table on a silver tray, with a jug of ice cold water from the burn, and had a tea towel draped over his left arm.

"Are you enjoying your stay lads?" he asked them.

The servicemen agreed the craic was good and they were enjoying their few days' leave in such lovely surroundings.

One of the lads asked, "Who is the poor lady in the room next to ours? She was crying all night, she sounded so upset."

McKillop froze. "You are the only guests this week, you must be mistaken."

Two or three of the lads spoke up – "Yes, we have heard her too, and we saw her last night walking along the corridor, she was wearing a green dress and looked very sad."

"That's right," said another. "I saw her walking out on the lawn yesterday evening, just before dusk, I'm sure she was weeping."

In all the years McKillop had worked there, he'd never seen her, but he knew a number of reliable people who had.

Well, who *is* she?" one of the soldiers asked."

When he saw that they were not going to let it go, he decided to tell them the curious story of 'The Green Lady of Mamore.'

"Her name is Lady Grace McLeod. She and her husband, Major Harris McLeod, were married in St Paul's Cathedral in London in 1914 and honeymooned here at Mamore Lodge, just months before World War 1 broke out.
Major McLeod was called back to Barracks and he and his regiment were sent over to Northern France, where he and 23 of his Regiment lost their lives due to a dreadful Gas attack.
When Grace heard the news, she was heartbroken.
Later that year, she gave birth to a baby boy who she called Torquil, but misfortune was to visit her once more – as the poor wee mite took ill and died at 6 months old.
Poor Grace was inconsolable – and she took her own life, such was her distress."
"Oh dear!" said one of the servicemen. "How sad…" and there was a silence as they all felt the pain and sorrow.

"Yes, and it is said that the 'Green Lady' still walks these corridors at night, looking for her dear Harris and her child."

The silence was almost tangible as the battle hardened servicemen sat in sombre mood.

McKillop knew that these men had endured the most atrocious conditions in the trenches and witnessed the most appalling scenes in battle.

But there they were, bereft at the sad plight of Lady Grace McLeod.

After a few minutes, one of the lads said in a more cheerful voice. "I think this calls for another dram! McKillop, if you please."

This was met with a cheer – and McKillop fetched another round of 'Uisge Beatha,' the water of life, for the thirsty servicemen.

"These are on the house!" McKillop said, such was his admiration for these hardy lads.

Another cheer went up.

The lads spent the rest of the night sharing ghost stories, some of which were true accounts and others which were mischievously made up for the devilment of it.

The next morning, breakfast was a quiet affair, until someone mentioned the Green Lady.
"Did anyone see the Green Lady last night? One lad said mischievously.
No-one admitted to seeing her, but one of the group said, "No, but I definitely heard someone crying in the room next to ours, last night."
Silence enveloped the room as they looked uneasily at each other.
"Well, I for one don't believe in all that 'Green Lady' rubbish. It's just a story made up for the tourists!" One of the group said.
Others tentatively nodded in agreement.

"Come and look at this," said one of the lads who was looking out of the window. "There's something lying on the ground down there."
There was a scramble as they all made for the door and ran down the stairs.
"Look!" said one as he pointed at a shawl which was lying on the newly fallen snow.

"It's a shawl - a *green* shawl!"

"Yes, and look there!" – there was a single line of footprints in the snow, leading from the back door, across the yard, disappearing into the bracken.

"They look like a child's footprints, they're very small," someone said.

"That, or a young woman's footprints!"

"You don't think…. ?"

The Sergeant saw that some of the younger lads were shaking.

"Come on lads, let's go back inside." He said as he ushered them inside. "The brochan *(porridge)* will be getting cold."

As they were seated, someone asked, "Did anyone pick up the shawl?"

They realised that in their haste to get in out of the cold, the shawl had been left lying.

"Cochrane, go down and bring up the shawl," the Sergeant said.

"Yes Sarge," Corporal Cochrane replied and went down to see.

Within a few minutes, he returned. "Sir… the em… the shawl isn't there. I looked all around, it's definitely not there. And…" he hesitated, "neither are the footprints, gone they are, gone."

"What do you mean 'they're not there?' Did we not see them with our very own eyes?"

"Yes Sarge but, but… they're not there now."

The men dashed over to the windows and looked out.

"He's right, Sarge," one of them said. "They're gone!"

The rest of the breakfast was taken in silence as a heavy snowfall covered the ground.

But each of them knew what they had seen…

They were just finishing their breakfast when the local Bobby, walked in.

"Hello boys," he said. "Police Constable Malcom at your service.

I heard you were staying here for a few days, and I thought I would come up and say, 'Hello' and thank you for your service against the Hun. We feel safer knowing that you lads are out there, serving King and Country, keeping us safe back home. And if there's anything I can do, please don't hesitate to ask."

"That's very kind of you, Constable," Sergeant McKinnon replied. "But everything is just grand, isn't it, lads?"

"Unless you want to stand us all a dram!" One of the lads said cheekily. The boys laughed but Sergeant McKinnon was not amused.

"That's enough, young McGhee! I apologise Constable, but the boys are just back from the front line and are a bit high spirited."

"Don't you be worrying, there's no harm done and I would be only too pleased to stand my hand" *(buy a round).*

A great cheer went up and Bookem gave McKillop £3, saying, "That's for a bottle of whisky for the lads, keep the change. It's a bit early in the day just now, so keep it until tonight."

"Will do," McKillop replied.

"Anything else boys?" Bookem asked.

"Well, maybe you can explain this business about the Green Lady?" Sergeant McKinnon asked. "Some of the lads say they have seen her, what do you make of it?"

"Well, I don't know what I can say, except that I have never seen her myself, but I know a few people who have."

"So you don't believe she exists?" one of the group asked Bookem.

"I'm not saying that. There are many things I don't understand but then perhaps we are not meant to *'understand'* them." Bookem had a very open opinion on such things.

"Well, some of the lads are going to lie in wait for her tonight and confront her."

"Oh no! Don't be doing that!" Bookem said with conviction. "You shouldn't be concerning yourselves with such things, things that are beyond our understanding. You never know what harm you might unleash. Please don't be meddling lads."

"We've faced the guns of the Hun, aye, and their hellish gas too, there's nothing on this earth that can frighten us now, Constable," replied one of the soldiers.

"But this may *not* be of *this* earth. Please be careful, be very careful." Bookem said with sincere concern. "It's not wise to interfere in such things.

Anyway, I'd better get going, I have an appointment with a class of children in 10 minutes. Take care, boys – catch up with you later."

Bookem jumped into his Land Rover and bumped his way down the track to the main road below, and on to the school.

He enjoyed talking to the children about his work. You never knew what they might come away with, or what questions they would ask.

His talk that day was about not accepting lifts from strangers.

"Be careful now, don't be getting into cars with strange people," was his message.

"My dad says that my Uncle Angus is a bit strange – should I not be going in the car with him?" asked young Kirsty Macneill.
"Well, er… um…that's different" Bookem said.
"How is it different?" Kirsty wasn't going to be put off so easily.
"Well….. is Uncle Callum a stranger?" Bookem asked.
'No, but he has one blue eye and one green eye. My dad says that he supports Rangers and Celtic at the same time! My granny always laughs when my dad says that."

"Gosh, look at the time!" Bookem said. "I have a very important undercover case to detect, so I have to go now, children. Take care, keep safe and remember, don't be taking lifts from people you don't know."
"Does that include the new Minister?" Kirsty was persistent. "My grannie says he's very strange…she hides behind the settee when she sees him come up the path."
Just for a fleeting moment, Bookem considered making a run for it – but he composed himself

and said with a forced smile, "Bye, children," and left the assembly at speed.

Returning to the safety of the Police station, he put on the kettle and thought to himself, 'My, but the children are getting smarter every year, I'm sure!"

As he sipped his tea and enjoyed a Custard Cream biscuit, his mind went back to his conversation with the lads at Mamore Lodge earlier in the day.
He thought to himself ~ *"They wouldn't confront the Green Lady, would they? But they had been to hell and had come back, seen more horrors than any of us could ever imagine, maybe they would seek her out.*
'I'd better go up to Mamore Lodge tonight and see what's what."

It was 9 pm when Bookem pulled up outside Mamore Lodge. He could hear boisterous singing coming from the Bar area, followed by cheers and laughter.

'The boys seem to be enjoying themselves,' Bookem thought to himself as he walked in the front entrance and made his way through to the Bar.

There was a great cheer when he walked in – "Look out boys, it's the long arm of the law!" someone shouted, and another cheer was given.

"Okay lads, calm down," Bookem said with good humour, which only caused the lads to give an even louder cheer.

Bookem could see that he wasn't going to get anywhere tonight, so he ordered a dram and sat down next to Sergeant McKinnon.

"They are in good spirits tonight, Sergeant, what's the occasion?" Bookem asked.

"Oh, they don't usually need a special occasion, Constable, but we are returning back to the barracks tomorrow, and then off to the front again, so they're enjoying their last night of freedom."

Bookem fell silent. What could he say? He knew that some of them wouldn't return home to their loved ones.

Such a mad, sad, waste of life.

Just then, a voice shouted, "Who's for chatting up the Green Lady?" Another cheer went up.

Bookem urged them to forget about the Green Lady and have another dram, but they were determined to find her, and a number of them got up and went to search the corridors.
"Come on lads, I'll stand my hand (*buy a round of drinks*) shouted Sergeant McKinnon – but they were not to be deterred.

The saying, '*They were making enough noise to wake the dead,*' was particularly appropriate that night, as they charged around the hotel corridors, shouting and calling out her name.
Bookem felt sure that the 'Green Lady,' if the stories were to be believed, would certainly not appear with such a hullabaloo going on. After half an hour or so, the soldiers returned to the Bar, which McKillop had now closed – he had found the whole business to be in very bad taste and had locked up the Bar and turned in.
"No drink – and no Green Lady – it's too bad! one of the lads said, and many of them agreed.

Sergeant McKinnon ordered them all to go to bed as they had an early start the next morning, then there was the drive back to Barracks in Inverness.

There were a few grumbles as they made their way to bed.

"What time are you leaving in the morning, Sergeant? Bookem asked.

"7 am, bright and breezy – and any stragglers will be left behind."

"I'll come up and wish them all well," Bookem said.

He knew that they were good lads, it was the drink that had a hold of them, or perhaps a fear of what might lie ahead for them – would they make it home after the war? Would they see their loved ones again?

Yes, they were good lads in a bad situation.

True to his word, Bookem was waiting in the reception area the next morning at 6.45.

He shook hands with each soldier as they passed him, and said to each one, "Thank you, take care, and may the good Lord bless you. Sorry, there was no Green Lady, lads – maybe next time!"

The lads scrambled into the truck, looking bleary-eyed and seriously hungover.

Bookem waved them off and climbed into his Land Rover.

Just as he was about to move off, he turned to wave to McKillop, who was standing at the main entrance, when he saw a figure in the upstairs bedroom window.

It was Lady Grace McLeod, wearing a Green dress, and she held a handkerchief to her eye. Perhaps she was remembering when she waved her dear husband, Major Harris McLeod, off to the front some years ago, but he was never to return.......

Bookem smiled, gave her a nod of respect and drove down the steep hill to the Police station to pour himself a large dram, just to steady his nerves.

The Mamore Lodge, high in the Hills above Kinlochleven.

'The Curious Case of the Seer of Tullamore'

8.

A few years ago, a small group of friends came over from County Offaly, in the south of Ireland, looking for 'a start' on the road squads in Scotland. It was the time of the Hydro schemes and road building across the West Coast of Scotland and there were great opportunities for those who weren't afraid of hard graft.

County Offaly is a beautiful, rural area, and is known for having a number of 'thin places' where this world and the 'other world' have only a thin veil between them.

The youngest 'lad' was called Seamus O'Mally who was no more than 17 years old. He had always been a polite child but was also an odd boy, very different from the other children in his school in the village of Tullamore.

He was a bit of a loner, and if anyone wanted to find him, he could usually be found sitting beside the clear waters of the 'Corrie Burn,' on the edge of his village, looking for unusual stones to collect and add to his already sizeable collection.

So far, his collection included several grey stones with white stripes through them, a number of pure white stones, an azure blue stone, three shiny black stones, a large jade stone and several red stones, which he only touched when wearing gloves, as it is well known that red stones are bad luck!

The other children would occasionally sneak up behind him and were sure they often heard him speaking with the babbling waters as it made its way down- stream.

They never knew what he was saying as he spoke in a language they had never heard before. They knew for sure that it wasn't their native Gaelic tongue, or the *Béarla, the English*, that the teachers insisted the children spoke when in school.

As he grew up, the locals called him Seamus *'the Seer'* O'Mally.

His uncle Patrick, *aka Paddy Gallacher*, had found work on the roads on the Island of Mull, which included renewing large tracts of road between Lochdon and Bunessan, as well as bridge building over the many burns *(streams)* they encountered along the way.

Like so many of the Irish navvies, Paddy had written home and encouraged family and friends to come over to the West of Scotland, as there was plenty of work to be had.

A new jetty was built at the Fishnish Ferry, near Salen, which often meant working through the night or as the various tides dictated.

One man had already lost his life due to the strong and fast moving currents there.

To be fair, by the time many of the lads turned up for the night shift, a vast amount of alcohol had already been consumed, and such tragedies were inevitable.

The lads were billeted in roughly constructed wooden huts, each one housed six workers.

They came from 'all the airts' – the Islands, Glasgow, West Coast villages and, of course, Ireland - a diverse mix!

Stories would be told well into the night, and much alcohol was taken as the dim tilly lamps flickered and made strange shapes and images on the hut walls – much to the anxiety of the younger lads!

The quality of the stories depended on the skill of the storyteller – and the amount of 'uisge' (whisky) consumed!

Young Seamus O'Mally never really fitted into the life of a Navvy, but his 'gift' was well respected (*feared?*) by his fellow Irishmen, and he was left in peace most of the time. It wasn't long after arriving on Mull that his gift of prophecy became apparent.
One night, he had a 'dream' in which he saw a Thunderstorm followed by a 'rainstorm of rocks.'

"Raining Rocks?" his uncle Patrick said, "Whatever on earth does that mean?"

"I don't know, Uncle," he answered, "but I see a dark cloud and have a feeling of great fear."

Later that day, a van came racing down to the Office hut at Craignure. It was Donnie McDonald *(aka the Moon Man, so called because of his strange behaviour on the night of the full moon, or so it is said)* with news that there had been an explosion as the men were clearing away the rocks where a bridge foundation was to be laid.

A young lad from Cork had been caught in the explosion and was killed as the rocks were blown up into the air, and then rained down upon him, effectively stoning him to his death.

Some weeks later, Seamus told his uncle Paddy that he had a dream where he saw a river burst its banks and two large trees were flowing down stream. Paddy told Seamus not to say a word to anyone about it, for the fear it might spread.

That very night, a group of lads were shoring up the boarding at the new Fishnish Ferry site, when, after a few days of heavy rain, the scaffolding on which they were standing was swept away, and two men were carried down stream.

It was a few weeks later, that their bodies were found. on the shoreline at Lochaline on the Morven peninsula, across the Sound of Mull from the Fishnish Ferry.

Word got out that Seamus had 'seen' the tragic event before it happened. Many of the other Navvies kept clear of Seamus after that.

There were even those who didn't believe that Seamus had 'the gift' at all, and had been, in some way, responsible for the recent deaths.

As the rumour mill gained strength, young Seamus was shunned and snubbed by many of the other navvies. It got so bad that Donnie McDonald called Paddy Gallacher to come to the office.

"What's going on with young Seamus, Paddy? The boys aren't happy, and they're wanting me to send him down the road (sack him) before someone else gets killed."

"He's just a boy, Donnie. He's well known in his home village for having 'the gift,' but there's no harm in him."

"Maybe not, Paddy, but I can't have bad feeling in the camp, it's not good for morale – and that will only lead to more trouble among the lads." Donnie replied. "Well, if he were to be cleared by the Polis, would that not stop the tongues wagging? After all, if they're suggesting it's tantamount to murder, then we'd have no choice but to call the local Bobby to investigate, would we?"

"Mmm, that's an idea Paddy. I know the local Sergeant in Tobermory. I met him a few years back, when he was the local Bobby in Ballachulish – and we were on Islay at the same time too. He's a good man, known as 'Bookem,' he's quite a character." So, it was agreed that Donnie would go down to Tobermory and talk it over with Bookem to see what he could advise.

It was 7 am the next morning, and 'Bookem,' was just finishing stirring his porridge when the doorbell of the Tobermory Police station rang.

"Who on earth is up and about at this early hour?" Bookem said to himself. At the door stood a rough, tough kind of a man who held out his hand and said, "I am sorry to disturb you at this ungodly hour…, oh, but where are my manners? I am…" Before he could continue, Bookem interrupted him and said, "Hello Donnie, it's good to see you again. How are you?"

"I wasn't sure that you would remember me, it's been a few years since we last met. We were on Islay at the same time, if I remember." Donnie said and smiled, which is something he didn't often do.

"That's right Donnie – do you remember thon young lassie who said she had a friend that no-one else could see? That was a strange business with the Rag doll, wasn't it?

"Aye, it was that." Donnie replied.

"Anyway, come away in, the kettle had just boiled."

They spent a while recalling incidents and characters which they had both known. "But I'm sure you didn't come to talk about old times – what can I do for you, Donnie?"

"Well, there's been a couple of incidents which are causing much unrest at the camp up at Craignure," Donnie explained.

"Many of the boys are superstitious..." and he went on to explain about the two recent deaths and how a number of the workers blamed a lad called Seamus O'Mally and his apparent ability to 'see' things before they happened.

"They say that Seamus had a hand in it, but I've spoken to him and I'm not so sure. I'm afraid there might be trouble and wondered if you would come up and see what you can make of it before things get out of hand."

"Of course I will, Donnie, but I have a 'surprise' spot check later this morning at 10 o'clock, when Sgt Galbraith is coming off the Oban ferry – but I'll come up after that, say 12 o/clock, would that suit?"

"That's just grand, Book.... em, yes, that will be fine, Sergeant Malcolm," Donnie said as he left the room.

At 12.15 exactly, Bookem walked into the site hut at Craignure. "You're in good time, Sergeant," Donnie said. "I wasn't expecting you for a while yet."

(It is worth saying that Time, on the West Coast of Scotland, has a certain amount of 'slippage' built into any arrangements. For example, if you arrange to meet someone at, say, 10 am, you wouldn't expect them to arrive until at least 10.15 or even 10.30.

As my grandmother used to say, "When the good Lord made time, He made plenty of it...so what's the hurry?"

Back in the site hut, Bookem asked, "Is the lad here?"

"Aye, he's waiting in the office. Just go through."

Bookem walked into a small office and saw a young boy, looking very nervous. He took a seat and said, "Now, young Simon, don't you be worrying."

"Seamus," the boy said.
"Seamus?" Bookem replied.

"Aye, Seamus, not Simon."
"Since when?" Bookem asked.
"Since the very day I was Baptised, sir."
"Well, who's Simon O'Mally?"
"I'm sure I don't know, sir."
"So, who is this Seamus O'Mally then?" Bookem was getting more confused by the minute. "Me, sir. *I'm* Seamus O'Mally.
"Are you sure?" Bookem asked.
"Of course, I'm sure."
"Well, why didn't you say so sooner? Okay, Seamus, or whatever you're calling yourself nowadays, what's all this about? I hear that you had a hand in the deaths of two men. What do you have to say for yourself?"

"Not me sir! But I *do* have the 'sight' and can see some things before they happen – and it's a curse, to be sure." Seamus replied, on the verge of tears.

"Mmmm, that's very convenient – so you *abscond* yourself from all responsibility for their deaths?"

"I do that. I wish I didn't see such things! It's a terrible burden on me." The tears were rolling down the boy's cheeks and Bookem could see that he was genuinely distressed.

Bookem had seen such cases before. He knew Sandy McLean, in Dervaig, who was known as 'The Seer of Dervaig,' who also had 'the sight' and was so often greatly disturbed by some of the things he had 'seen'.

After a few more minutes of chatting, Bookem could see that young Seamus was no murderer.

He called Donnie McDonald into the office and told him that he was quite sure that Seamus had no hand in the deaths. It was his opinion that the loss of life was due to 'unknown accidental reasons, aggravated by the taking of too much whisky.'

Word soon got around that young Seamus was found not guilty of the two deaths, but there were still a few navvies who were not convinced and kept him at arm's length.

Life got pretty much back to normal for a while. Seamus started collecting his stones in the burns again – and he kept his dreams to himself.

After a few months, however, Seamus had the most terrible 'dream.' His uncle Paddy asked what was troubling him, but he remained silent.

Seamus was in a dark mood for some weeks, and then, one night, he disappeared. Paddy asked around but no one had seen him for some time.

Donnie McDonald told Paddy that Seamus had said he was, *'going home.'*

Later the next day, it was reported, by some of the lads working on the Fishnish Ferry, that they had found a pair of boots tied together by the laces and hanging over the branch of a tree. On inspection, the boots were found to contain a number of red stones. (*And as we know, red stones are bad luck*). Paddy recognised the boots as belonging to Seamus.

Sergeant Bookem was called in to investigate the sorry business - and after talking to Donnie McDonald, Paddy Gallacher and some of the lads who had worked with Seamus, he concluded that Seamus had been very low in spirits and it was possible that he had died by his own hand. Bookem recorded his sad passing as 'death by misadventure' – to save the family any more distress than was necessary.

A few days after, Seamus's dear mother, Mary O'Mally, received a telegram which said, *"Sad news, stop. Seamus believed to have been called to the Lord, stop. He is now at rest. Stop. Patrick. Stop."*

But *was* he dead, or had he simply disappeared? If so, where had he gone? Would he reappear one day? We may never know, but our hope is that wherever Seamus is now, *'The Seer of Tullamore,'* will find a peace in death that had eluded him in life.

*

P.S. A number of years later ~ when Paddy was in his 70's ~ and his health wasn't good due to too many years of hard graft on the Roads, the Hydro schemes and various other building sites.

He had to go to Dublin for a hospital appointment, and because of the distance between Tullamore and Dublin *(About 50 miles or so)*, and there only being one bus a day, Paddy decided to take lodgings for a couple of nights in the 'Fair city.' It was a good opportunity to catch up with some of his old Navvy pals and swap a few tales with them.
They agreed to meet in the Temple Bar, beside the River Liffey – and a few glasses of 'Liffy

Water' (aka Guinness) were taken – in moderation, of course. As the evening wore on, the tales got more outrageous, and the craic was good.

About 10 pm, a grubby, scruffy looking 'Traveller' shuffled into the Bar, offering to tell individual fortunes if they would, 'cross his palm with Silver.'

The lads called him over to their table for the craic, and Paddy gave him a silver coin and held out his hands, palms upwards.

"Well, my boy, am I to be a millionaire by next week?" Paddy said, and the others laughed.

The boy froze and became extremely anxious. Paddy took a closer look and saw that the traveller had a large mole on his left cheek, just as his young nephew Seamus had."Who are you!?" Paddy asked as he grabbed his wrist.

"Let me go, Paddy," he shouted, "Let me go!" "How do you know my name? Seamus, is it yourself?" Paddy shouted. The Traveller made such a fuss that the Landlord came over and insisted that Paddy let him go at once.

In the melee, the Traveller managed to get free and made for the door.
Paddy jumped up and followed him out, but the night was dark and he was nowhere to be seen.
Paddy, desperate to find him, called out, "Seamus, Seamus my lad, come back!" But the Traveller had disappeared into the night.

When Paddy returned to the table, next to his Pint of Guinness, was a piece of green jade, about the size of a Walnut.

Paddy's friend looked and said, "A green stone! A sign of good luck and healing. How did that get there?"

But Paddy knew who had left it, his favourite nephew, Seamus O'Mally from Tullamore.

Some weeks later, when Paddy received his test results from the Hospital, it was found that the tumour that his G.P. had diagnosed had completely gone, and he was given a clean bill of health.

Paddy closed his eyes and said, "Thank you, Seamus, and may the good Lord bless you, wherever you are," and a tear ran down his cheek.

Poor Seamus was never seen again.

A sad business, to be sure.

'The Curious Case of The Little Rag Doll'

9.

Foreword : This story is not a 'case' in the true sense of a 'Police case,' however, Bookem assured me that it is a true story in which he played a small part and is well worth telling.

The beautiful island of Islay, also known as 'The Queen of the Hebrides', is the southernmost of the Inner Hebridean islands and lies off the West coast of Scotland. Along with the neighbouring island of Jura, it's known for its distinctive peaty flavoured Whiskies (Bookem's favourite tipple).

It has been called 'The land of Whisky, Geese and Ghosts.'

Fortuitous finds indicate that it has been occupied since as early as 8,000 BC.

Here is a tale from that delightful Island, which Bookem assured me is true – it happened while he was the local Bobby there.

It concerns a young family, the Wrights, who moved up to Islay from the South.

John, Dorothy, son Benjamin, who was aged 9, and young Charlotte, aged 5, were all excited with their new life in the Scottish Islands.

John had secured the head Chemist's position at one of the Distilleries, Dorothy was a Nursery Teacher and hoped to be able to help out at the local school, and the children were settling in at the local Primary school.

They had purchased a large house near Bunnahabhain (*Boona-haaven*), and they soon settled down into Island life.

A few weeks after they moved in, Dorothy noticed that Charlotte was becoming quite withdrawn. She didn't seem to have many friends, and as Dorothy walked by her bedroom, she often heard little Charlotte talking to herself – or so it seemed.

She spoke to John about it, and he said that it was probably a phase she was going through and would grow out of it in time.

Dorothy wasn't so sure.

A few days later, she was waiting for Benjamin and Charlotte outside the school when Constable Malcolm, aka 'Bookem,' came out, having given the children a talk about the dangers of talking to strangers.

"Oh, hello, you must be Mrs Wright, am I right?" Bookem said with a mischievous smile. Dorothy smiled and said, "Yes, and you must be Constable Malcolm." Dorothy replied.

"Indeed, I am. Are you all settling in alright?"

"Yes, thank you, it's a beautiful Island, and the locals are ever so kind. People have been popping in with soup and scones and the like."

"Och, that's good, yes, they are very friendly folk. Where are you staying?" Bookem asked.

"We bought the 'big house', on the outskirts of Bowmore on the Gartbreck road. It's a lovely spot."

Bookem said, in a sombre tone, "Oh, so you're in the 'Big House,' is everything alright?"

Dorothy sensed a change in Bookem's tone. "Yes, everything is just fine, why wouldn't it be?"

"Oh, er, no reason. Gosh, is that the time? I'll have to go. I hope to catch up with Mr Wright and the family, before too long. I'd better be away. Take care now." And Bookem jumped into his Land Rover and drove off.
Dorothy was left feeling that something wasn't right – something was left unsaid – but whatever could it be?

That evening, as Dorothy was passing Charlotte's bedroom, she heard her speaking to someone. As she listened, Charlotte was saying, "There, there, don't cry so – I'll help you, don't worry."
Dorothy opened the bedroom door hastily and looked around. Charlotte was sitting on the bed talking to *herself*.
"Who are you speaking to, sweetheart?" Dorothy asked.
"My friend, Ailsa."

"But... but where _is_ your friend?"

"She's sitting on the end of the bed, silly, can't you see her?"

Dorothy was becoming uneasy, and if she was totally honest, she was more than a little anxious, too.

"Ok, Charlotte, dinner is almost ready, come downstairs, and remember to wash your hands."

"Ok mummy, I'll just say goodbye to Ailsa."

Dorothy didn't mention it to John, he would only say it was a figment of Charlotte's imagination, but she felt it was something more than that.

Dinner was a strained affair, Dorothy was not going to mention Charlotte's little 'friend,' not yet anyway – and she hoped that Charlotte wouldn't either.

"How did you get on at school today sweetheart?" John asked Charlotte.

"It was great daddy! And I've made a new friend, too."

"That's good…"
"Yes, her name is Ailsa."
Dorothy froze. "Don't be bothering daddy, eat up your dinner or it will go cold."
"But mummy, it's a salad!"

Dorothy spent the next week or two worrying about Charlotte and her 'new friend.' So much so that she felt she really needed to talk to someone about it.
She didn't know anyone well enough to share it with, then she remembered Constable Bookem.
She phoned him that afternoon and they arranged a meeting for the next day, when her husband was at work and Benjamin and Charlotte were in school.

"It's good of you to come at such short notice, Constable Book…em, Malcolm."
 "It's no bother, Mrs Wright."
"Please, call me Dorothy."
"Thank you, em, Dorothy. What seems to be bothering you? I hope everything is alright.

Everyone is so pleased that we have a nice family in the 'big house' again."

She explained all that had happened with Charlotte and Ailsa, while Bookem listened intently.

"Oh dear. There's something you should know which might explain a few things – um – Dorothy.

Many years ago, a rich family, called the Armstrongs, who had moved up from the Borders, once owned this house.

Mr Armstrong owned much of the land we see around us and employed a number of locals on his land.

He was cruel and vindictive. He once sacked a man for not doffing his cap as he walked by and threw him and his family out of their croft. They were reduced to begging for food. Sadly, their youngest daughter wandered off and was never found.

"How awful!" Dorothy said. "Her poor mother must have been beside herself with worry."

"And it might surprise you to know that the

poor child was called…" Bookem hesitated, "… Ailsa."

"Oh my goodness, how strange!" Dorothy said,

Whatever was going on? Was it just coincidence – or was there more to it than meets the eye? If so, then what? Dorothy was more confused than ever.

She decided she would speak to her husband, John, about it when he got in from work that evening.

Later, when they had finished dinner that night, Dorothy sent Charlotte upstairs to her room to play with her dolls.

Charlotte reluctantly went to her bedroom, but not without making it quite clear that 'it wasn't fair!' as she climbed the stairs.

Dorothy then explained to John everything about Charlotte's new friend. She was quite sure it was much more than a mere coincidence that the girl's name was Ailsa.

John was quite surprised, "Goodness me, I didn't realise she was taking it so seriously! I just thought that Charlotte had an imaginary friend, as many children do, and that she would grow out of it in time. And what about poor Ailsa? How tragic."

"Could it be the same little girl that Charlotte talks to? But how could that even be possible?" Dorothy said.

Just a week or so ago, she had been quite sure that it was all in Charlotte's head, but now, well, she wasn't so sure.

"So, where do we go from here?" She asked John.

"Maybe we should ask Benjamin if he has heard anything at school," John suggested.

Just at that, young Benjamin ran in from visiting a friend.

"Ah, Benjamin, would you come in here for a minute, please?" John called.

"It wasn't me, I didn't do it!" Benjamin said in his own defence.

"What didn't you do?" John asked.

"Whatever it is you think I did! It was that Mark McNeil. The teacher says he is a wee besom. What's a besom daddy?" *(See footnote 1).*
"I'm sure I don't know, " said his father.
"We wanted to ask you – how is Charlotte getting on at school, has she got any friends?"
"They all think she is a bit weird. She talks to an imaginary friend all the time. Someone called, Elsie, or something like that. It's so embarrassing."
"Is the name, Ailsa?"
"Yes, that's it, Ailsa."
"Okay Benjamin, you can go up to your room now, and thank you."

"It's 'Ben' now, Dad, not Benjamin. That's what my new friends call me, they say Benjamin is too posh."

John thought Dorothy was going to have a fit.

"What!? Benjamin is your name and it's Benjamin that you will be called! I'll speak to Mr Cunningham, the Headmaster *(the children*

called him 'Foxy') in the morning and make sure you get your proper name.
Ben indeed!" Dorothy wasn't happy.
"Mum! Don't say anything to Foxy, he'll show me up in front of my friends! Pleeease!"
"Benjamin, go to your room!" John said sternly.
"Oh, alright," Benjamin mumbled as he went up the stairs.

"Maybe we should talk to Charlotte now and see if we can make some sense of it all. Perhaps she heard about it in school, although it seems unlikely. Let's call her down and see what she has to say."
"Good idea." Dorothy agreed and called up to Charlotte, "Will you come down, sweetheart? Daddy and I would like to speak to you about something."
"Am I in trouble?" Charlotte asked as she entered the kitchen.
"No, darling, don't worry, you haven't done anything wrong. It's about your friend, Ailsa. Can you tell us about her? She sounds very interesting."

"Oh, she's lovely, but always so sad. I first heard her crying one night and called out to her, and there she was, sitting at the end of my bed!"

"Were you not frightened, sweetheart?" John asked.

"No, daddy, she talks to me about her mummy and daddy, and about a horrible man who was cruel to them. But she wants me to be her friend, is that alright? I won't get into trouble, will I?"

"Of course not, darling," Dorothy and John said in unison.

"Do you know *why* she cries so?" John asked.

"She misses her mummy. She has looked for her but doesn't know where she is. Can we help her find her mummy, can we, can we, pleeease? She is _so_ sad."

John and Dorothy looked at each other – what could they say?

"I don't know what we _can_ do, sweetheart," Dorothy said, which brought a flood of tears from Charlotte. "

"Oh, please, please, mummy, pleeeeease."

It was enough to melt your heart.

"Has she said anything about where her mummy might be?" John asked.

"No, but she *did* say that she misses her mummy pushing her on the swing that her daddy made for her in a place where there were lots of silver trees, and black and white birds, but I don't know where that is."

John and Dorothy looked at each other.

Dorothy raised her eyebrows and nodded at Charlotte, who was looking very sad, and whispered, *"Let's just play along and maybe she'll drop the whole thing soon."*

John nodded in agreement and replied, "All right. Let's go and look."

"Really daddy? Are we *really* going look for Ailsa's mummy? She'll be so happy!"

"Ok sweetheart, we'll go in the morning, but we can't promise anything."

"Can we take Ailsa too, can we?"

John reluctantly said, "Oh, alright then. Now, it's time for bed."

Once Charlotte was tucked up and fast asleep, Dorothy asked John, "Any idea where to start looking?"

"Charlotte said it was in a place where there were 'silver trees' and 'black and white' birds, but I haven't a clue where or what that might be," replied John.

"Maybe we should ask Constable Bookem," Dorothy said. "He's sure to know where there's a forest of 'silver trees,' if there is such a thing."

"Good idea, it's not too late, I'll call him just now," John said as he reached for the telephone.

John and Bookem agreed to meet outside the Round Church in Bowmore *(See footnote 2)* at 9 o'clock the following morning.

The next day, John, Dorothy, Benjamin and Charlotte (and Ailsa) jumped into the car and headed for the Round Church, where they found Bookem waiting for them as agreed. Charlotte was beyond excited.

Bookem said that he had a good idea where to start and told John to follow him.

On the way, Charlotte was laughing and giggling in the back seat.

"Who are you talking to, sweetheart?" Dorothy asked, guessing what her answer would be.

"Ailsa, of course, mummy," Charlotte replied. "She is so excited. Will we find her mummy?

"We'll see. Now, sit quietly while daddy's driving."

"Yes, mummy."

"She's away with the fairies," Benjamin said shaking his head, thinking that his little sister had lost the plot altogether.

After about 10 minutes, Bookem pulled over, lowered his car window and pointed to a small wood of Silver Birch trees, just across the road. John pulled in behind him.

"Ah, silver trees!" John and Dorothy said together, realising what Ailsa had meant.

Dorothy heard a noise in the trees and said excitedly, "Look, and black and white birds too!"

"Yes, Magpies, there are lots of them here," Bookem said. "This looks like a good place to start. Some of the trees here are hundreds of years old. I think we might be lucky."

John thought it was all getting a bit out of hand, after all, he wasn't *really* expecting to find a tree with a swing attached, it was all just to keep Charlotte happy.

Earlier that morning, Dorothy and John had agreed that they would wander around for a while and then say something like, *"Oh well, we've looked around, but it doesn't look like there's anything here, maybe Ailsa has found her mummy and had gone away with her,"* hoping it might put an end to Charlotte's fantasies.

They spent a while looking around for a swing or a rope among the silver birches, but found nothing, which was no great surprise to John and Dorothy.

"Oh well, we'd better head back," John said, feigning a disappointed look.

"Oh alright, I suppose we might as well," Dorothy agreed, looking disappointed.

As they were walking back to the car, Charlotte shouted, "Mummy. Mummy, Ailsa says she can see the tree where her swing was.

She's running over there, by the big holly bush. Her mummy is calling for her." Charlotte ran after her friend.

"Come back Ailsa, come back!" Charlotte shouted. "Don't go, you are my most special friend ever!" Charlotte was close to tears.

"Mummy, she's gone! My best friend has gone away…" Poor Charlotte was heartbroken.

Dorothy picked her up and held her close.

"Don't cry, my love, Ailsa is with her mummy, she'll be happy now, that's good isn't it?"

Charlotte grudgingly agreed.

"Yes, she's happy now – I can hear her laughing, but I miss her _so_ much already."

Dorothy and John looked at each other – they could hear a child laughing too.

It was like a fantasy dream, unreal yet somehow very real too. They could hear it for themselves – but how could that be?

"Okay, let's get home!" John said, feeling very uncomfortable, he had never experienced anything like it before.

John and Dorothy thanked Bookem for his help and drove back home.

Once they were in the house, Dorothy said, "I'll take her upstairs for a wee sleep, she's had a lot of excitement today. I'll sit with her for a while until she drops off."
"Okay, sweetheart." John was glad that it was all over.
'Maybe Charlotte can get on with her schoolwork now.' He thought as he mulled it all over.
Unable to make any rational sense of it all, he shook his head and picked up last week's Sunday Post to see what Oor Wullie was up to.

After a few minutes, Dorothy shouted down from Charlotte's bedroom – "John, will you come up here?"
"Yes, what is it?" he said as he climbed the stairs with Benjamin (aka *Ben* to his friends) following on behind.
As they walked into Charlotte's bedroom, John was stopped in his tracks.
"Look at this," Dorothy said as she held up

a small bundle of rags.

"I came up to make Charlotte's bed before we went out, and it wasn't here then, I'm sure of it, but here it is, lying on the bed."

"What on earth is it?" John looked puzzled.

Charlotte said, "It's Ailsa's favourite doll, her daddy made it for her."

"Now that she has found her mummy, she must have left it behind for me, wasn't that a nice thing to do, daddy?" and she took the little rag doll and cuddled it.

"Oh, em, yes sweetheart, it was a very nice thing to do."

John and Dorothy looked at each other with a puzzled expression.

"See, I told you she was my *special* friend, didn't I?"

"Yes... you did, darling." Dorothy and John had to agree.

"Girls!" Benjamin said, and he walked downstairs, shaking his head.

Then Charlotte said to her mother, "And I'm going to call her Ailsa, after my best friend," and she snuggled under the blankets with the biggest smile.

"Let her sleep for a while, she's had quite a morning," Dorothy said. As they went towards the stairs, they heard a tapping noise at the window.

They turned and looked……

It was a Magpie, peering at them through the bedroom window.

John and Dorothy looked at each other and froze. After a few surreal minutes, they went downstairs in silence, still not exactly sure what they had witnessed that morning.

Then Dorothy remembered something Bookem had said to her not long after they had moved on to Islay ~ *"You're in the Islands now, anything can happen!"* Well, he was right there!

Footnotes :
1. *A Besom is a type of broom or brush, made from twigs or Heather, usually associated with Witches. Also used to refer to an awkward or difficult person*

2. *The 'Round Church' is more properly called Kilarrow Parish Church. It was built in the form of a circle in 1767, so that the Devil couldn't hide in the corners, or so it is said.*

*

There are many tales of strange happenings in the Highlands and Islands of Scotland.
Are they Fact or Fiction? Tales or Tradition? Perhaps a bit of both.
It would be foolish to discard them out of hand as 'old wives' tales or 'foolish folklore'.

As William Shakespeare once said, *"There are more things in heaven and earth, Horatio, than are dreamt of in your philosophy."*
(Hamlet Act 1, Scene 5).

'A FINE ROMANCE'

10.

It was a grand day for an Island Wedding.

The sun was shining on the beautiful island of Islay. The rain was keeping off (so far), and the Wedding guests were resplendent in their best hats, frocks, kilts, and tweed jackets, with a sprig of white heather in their lapels for good luck.

Bookem was resplendent in his Ancient Malcolm tartan kilt and tie, white socks and a 'come and go' cap (*so called as it has a peak at the back as well as the front – like a Deerstalker – and you can never be sure if the wearer is coming or going!*).

For reasons which have always evaded me, the older ladies always wore black to a Wedding, black dresses, black hats and black looks.

Could it be that the *marriage experience* has given them a very different view of, 'wedded bliss?' The children were excited and chasing each other around the church, much to the annoyance of their grandmothers who were chastising them saying, "Behave yourselves, now, the Lord's house isn't a place for highjinks and carry-ons!"

Katy Nicholson was to marry Callum Fraser, and PC Bookem had been invited to the Wedding as a guest of the Groom's family.
Callum's father, Donald, was a Special Constable and had worked alongside Bookem on a number of cases on Islay, but today was a day for celebrating, enjoying and giving thanks.

Word had just got out that the Bride was on her way and everyone hurried into the Church, the Bride's family on the left, and the Groom's family on the right, according to local custom.
Characteristically, John took a seat near the back, not being family, but the Groom's mother told him that a seat had been kept for him near the front. John reluctantly moved forward and found that he was to be seated next to the Groom's Aunty Flora.
Aunty Flora was a tonic, full of life and didn't take herself, or life, too seriously.

She was thought, by some, to be 'overly vivacious' but she had known sadness too, as her first husband had been lost at sea some years before, while serving on the deep-sea Trawler, 'The Highland Dancer', (so named after the fascinating sea creature of the same name. *Google*).

She was good company, and Bookem was pleased that he had moved seats after all.
As Katy and her bridesmaids processed down the aisle, Bookem noticed that a tear ran down Flora's cheek.

'Perhaps she is remembering her own wedding to her late husband, the poor lassie,' Bookem thought to himself, and he gently touched her arm as a gesture of kindness and understanding.
Flora whispered, "Thank you, John, it's kind that you are," and kissed him on the cheek.
The ladies in the pew behind gave a *'did you see that!?'* kind of nod to each other.
"Aye, she's a fast worker, that one!" whispered Mrs McLeod to her friend, Mrs Chisholm.

Bookem always found weddings difficult, they reminded him of his first and only love, Mairi McLean from Bunessan.

They had been courting for most of their teenage years, and it was generally thought that one day they would be married. Indeed, they had often talked about it, but sadly, Mairi contracted Polio at the age of nineteen, and after several visits to Oban Hospital, her family sent her to a convalescent home in Glasgow, but complications had set in, and poor Mairi passed away two years later.
John was heartbroken and didn't look romantically at another woman again.

It was the push that he needed to fulfil his ambition to join the Police - and with his sister Ina's encouragement, he made enquiries and in due course he was accepted into the Argyllshire Constabulary (*later to become part of the Northern Constabulary*).

Cupid's loss was the Constabulary's gain, and he went on to have a long and distinguished career.

His kindness, sense of fair play and a strong sense of service to the community meant that he became well liked and well respected wherever he served.

Understandably, he found weddings difficult and avoided them whenever possible.
Having said that, he was finding Katy and Callum's wedding a delight – Flora, was, in part, responsible for that.

He was taken by her sense of humour and bright disposition - and she was attracted by his general aura of kindness and quiet strength. He was a man, she thought, that a woman would feel safe with – and not only that - his rugged good looks were a plus, too!
 During the ceremony, Flora's hand somehow found its way over to Bookem, and before he knew it, she was holding his hand.

He hadn't noticed just when or how she had managed it, but he felt pleasantly comfortable in her company and wasn't inclined to move his hand. They looked at each other and smiled.

Just then, the Minister asked, "*Does anyone here know of any reason why this man and this woman should not be joined together in Holy Matrimony? If so, you must declare it now or forever hold your peace.*"
Flora squeezed Bookem's' hand, which caused him to panic and take a fit of coughing which could only be pacified by a swig from Andrew Brown's hip flask, which had been kindly offered.

"Thank you, Andrew," Bookem said. "I think something must have gone down the wrong way!"
(*Andrew was the bride's uncle and had noticed Bookem and Flora holding hands*).
 "Don't you be worrying John, I can see that you have your hands full." Andrew said with a smile and a wink.

The ceremony went well. The Minister pronounced the Benediction in Gaelic and the Bride and Groom walked down the aisle to 'Mairi's Wedding' sung by the local Gaelic choir, of which both Katy and Callum were members.

It is a catchy tune (*'The Lewis Bridal Song'*) and the wedding guests found themselves dancing down the aisle.

It was a lovely end to a lovely Wedding Service. Bookem and Flora walked down the aisle arm in arm, which didn't go unnoticed by the village ladies.

"Didn't I tell you that one is a fast worker with the men?" Mrs McLeod whispered, "If she gets her way, she'll have Bookem down the aisle before Lambing time!"

Some of the ladies tut-tutted and others shook their heads.

All except Mrs MacPherson who said, "Well, good luck to them, I say. They have both known sadness, they deserve some happiness in their lives."

The other ladies reluctantly agreed as they walked away from the little Island church.

The Minister had overheard the ladies' conversation and said quietly to Mrs MacPherson as she walked by, "It's kind that you are Margaret. May the good Lord's blessings be with you."

Over the following weeks and months, it was not unusual to see Bookem and Flora 'walking out.'

What had once been a hot topic for the gossips, was now just old hat.

Inevitably, there were rumours of an impending Wedding.
"Well, they've been winching for a while now, it's time he made an honest woman of her," was just one of a number of comments that had been doing the rounds.
This was news to Bookem and Flora, they were simply enjoying each other's company and making the most of each day.

If the truth were to be told, it was a subject that Flora had often entertained in her solitary moments.

And so, one starlit evening, as they walked out to the 'Green Shed,' which was a small road workman's hut about 2 miles out of the village, Flora took a deep breath and said, "John, have you heard the rumours about you and me getting married?"
"I have heard some such thing, but I put it down to idle gossip. You know how some of the village ladies like to speculate."
"I do, John – but what if it wasn't *just* gossip?" Bookem was confused.
"But, but… we're *not* getting married – are we?" He added.
"Well, that's up to yourself John…" Flora's heart was beating ten to the dozen now. Was she being too forward?
"Do you mean?........"
"Yes John, I was wondering how you would feel if we were to, er, you know, 'become one.'
"Become one what?" He still hadn't clicked on.

"John," she said forcefully, "I am asking if you would marry me?"

He was caught completely off guard.
"Oh right, yes, married, right. Well, er, um, actually I…" And he fumbled in his pocket, got down on one knee and said, "I have been carrying this in my pocket for the last 2 months, just waiting for the right moment."
He opened a small box and took out a simple, yet beautiful engagement ring and said, "I bought this ring many years ago for the one I loved, and have kept all these years, would you be offended if I offered it to *you*, the one I love, and ask you - Flora, will you do me the great honour of becoming my wife?"
"Oh, John, it's a beautiful ring, and I would be honoured to wear it – and yes, of course I will marry you, you sly fox!"
As Bookem stood up she gave him a big hug as the tears of joy ran down her face.

Needless to say, the gossips had a field day when the news broke.

"See, I told you she was one for the men," said one.

"Aye, she's a fast one that!" said another.

But the news was welcomed by the majority of folks. They were pleased that the two of them had found happiness together.

A date was set and Bookem wrote to his good friend, the Reverend Colin Campbell, who was the Minister on the Inner Hebridean Island of Rhua – asking him if he would be so kind as to conduct their Wedding ceremony.

They had shared many a scrape in his time as the local Bobby on Rhua and he could think of no better man to ask.

In due course, Reverend Campbell replied and said he would be honoured to carry out the service for them.

On the set date, Colin, his wife Lorna and daughter Fiona attended.

It was a great day, with family and friends over from the mainland as well as the many locals who gathered outside the church.

John's brother, Archie, didn't keep good health but made the effort to be there, saying, "I just had to shake the hand of the woman who was brave enough to marry John!" with a warm smile.

John's sister, Ina, had sadly passed on three years prior.

The highlight, for the children, was the 'scramble' after the service, where pennies, thruppenny bits and a few sixpences were thrown from the car as the Bride and Groom left the church, and the children scrambled to see who could collect the most.

The wedding lasted 5 days in total, what with the pre-wedding celebrations, the Wedding Day itself and the post-wedding merriment.

Young men in kilts were seen wandering around the village for days, all in varying stages of disarray and sobriety.

A few days after the Service, someone had asked one of the local lads how the wedding had gone, and he replied, "Fine – so far!"

The 'happy couple' enjoyed a long and happy marriage – and they gave thanks to God everyday for blessing them and bringing them together.

John and I took pleasure in our friendship, and we continued to meet regularly in the Mishnish for a dram and a blether, indeed, it was during these chats that I gleaned information to write these stories.

I was pleased to meet Flora, aka Mrs Malcolm, on many occasions and always found her to be good company.

It was quite apparent that she thought the world of John, and he felt the very same about Flora.

And I am quite sure they were right, they most certainly *had* been blessed by our good and gracious God.

*

Constable John Malcolm aka 'Bookem', passed into glory aged 97, in his home near Tobermory. He was well known and well liked across the Highlands and Islands of Scotland. He was a gentleman of the highest order and respected by all who knew him.

Flora tended his grave faithfully and visited there every morning without fail. She always left a small spray of flowers in his memory – until her own passing some years later, when she was laid to rest beside her dear John.

He was, without doubt, a good man and a good friend to many - and will be mourned for many years to come, here, on the beautiful Island of Mull, and beyond.

MAY HE REST IN HEAVENLY PEACE

THE END

I hope you enjoyed my Books (4 so far) and who knows – perhaps PC John 'Bookem' Malcolm might even make a return at some time in the future, but until then...

Take care and keep safe.

Slàinte mhòr agus

a h-uile beannachd dhuibh.

Good health and every good blessing to you.

*

Disclaimer ~

Many of these stories are based on true events, with an element of embellishment for the telling of them.
If you think it might be yourself that I am talking about in a particular story, then be sure that it is not, if you catch my drift.

Other titles from this Author

Tales of a Highland Minister

More Tales of a Highland Minister

Even More Tales of a Highland Minister

*

If you enjoyed these stories, could I ask you to take a few minutes to leave a review on both Facebook and/or Amazon so that others may be encouraged to read and enjoy them too?

Mar sin leibh
(Goodbye)

Iain

©Iain Ramsden 2025
ISBN : 978-1-918264-26-5